All Interviews were performed by Shaun McClure and Hilary Wells
Book Layout Design by Jason Redway
Edited by Alison Woodward and Rob Gregorczyk

Additional proofreading by Rosie Thornton
Cover Illustration by Mus Fatih Cetiner and Shaun McClure
Internal illustrations by Shaun McClure, and (It Ain't Half Hot Mum!) Robin Grenville-Evans

All Photographs used in this publication have been given to use with permission directly from the Interviewees or their agents.

All other photos are copyright free images

Special thanks to;
All the Interviewees and their respective agents and publicists,
All Model and Prop Photos for Space 1999, Blake's 7 and Alien are the copyright of Martin Bower, and used with permission,
The Cooper Hall Foundation, for permission to use an image of Jeremy Burnham,
Owen Carne for permission to use his personal photos of The Vapors,
Jim Burns for permission to use his illustrations,
The Josh Kirby Estate for permission to use his book covers.
Hitchhiker's Guide to the Galaxy group illustration © Simon Butler and used with permission.
Hitchhiker's Guide to the Galaxy "Babel Fish" image © Rod Lord and used with permission.
Woody Woodgate portrait (on drums) and Madness image – used with permission from Grace Fairchild @GVF.Official Instagram

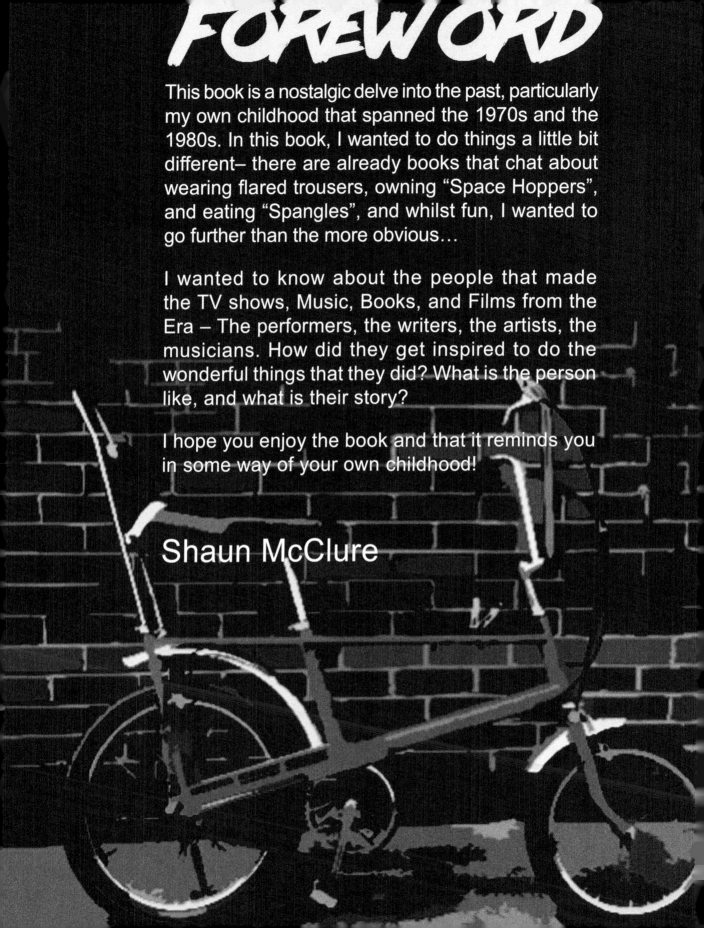

FOREWORD

This book is a nostalgic delve into the past, particularly my own childhood that spanned the 1970s and the 1980s. In this book, I wanted to do things a little bit different– there are already books that chat about wearing flared trousers, owning "Space Hoppers", and eating "Spangles", and whilst fun, I wanted to go further than the more obvious…

I wanted to know about the people that made the TV shows, Music, Books, and Films from the Era – The performers, the writers, the artists, the musicians. How did they get inspired to do the wonderful things that they did? What is the person like, and what is their story?

I hope you enjoy the book and that it reminds you in some way of your own childhood!

Shaun McClure

CONTENTS

BLUE PETER

Blue Peter celebrated its 60th anniversary in 2018! What I loved about Blue Peter was that when you watched the show, it seemed to be a positive version of what was happening on this side of the TV screen. There were people sitting on a sofa along with a couple of pets – quite normal friendly people.

On this side of the screen though, there was a dysfunctional family that definitely didn't want to chat to each other. So, we watched this nice surrogate family chat about their exciting lives – one moment making a Christmas decoration out of toilet rolls, and the next minute showing clips of that time they went Sky Diving.

It was at once bizarre and at the same time comforting... They seemed to exude calm but also a cheeky sense of humour. You felt like they were a part of your lives. If one of their pets died, we'd share in their grief - we really did. But we joined in with their fun too.

Peter Purves

Peter Purves was the presenter on the show during my formative years, and his partnerships with John Noakes and Valerie Singleton (and later, Lesley Judd) are rightly classed as the "Golden Age" of the show. He was the fun but sensible uncle opposite John, who was the eccentric one, whilst Valerie and Lesley kept it sensible but with a little wink to the camera once in a while.

Hilary: What sparked the original idea to become an actor? Didn't you want to be a teacher, originally?

Peter: No, I never wanted to be a teacher. I did become one, but I did that as a means of getting some sort of qualifications. I wanted to be an actor from the age of nine. I did the school play and that did it really. I played the lead in the first one, the second one and again in the third one so by the time I was 12, there was never any other option for me. I was used to doing stuff on stage.

I sang and I had quite a good boy soprano voice. My dad was a recording artist. Before his voice broke, he was one of the first people to record. He had his own teatime show on the BBC, in 1927 I think, so it was in the family. When his voice broke, he went into amateur dramatics and did Gilbert and Sullivan - that sort of stuff.

I grew up in Blackpool. What else are you going to do? You're either going to run a boarding house or go on the boards. I knew where I wanted to be and I was at school until I was 18 in Blackpool so I felt showbiz was in my blood really in some form-not because the family were involved particularly, although they were peripherally, it was just what people did. I knew that they could earn a living that way and that's what I wanted to do.

Shaun: You went from the stage into TV. How did that come about?

You always want to get into television. I didn't go to drama school. I decided not to teach anymore, I'd taught for a year so I was fully qualified. I said, "Right, I'm not doing that anymore," and

decided to wear out a bit of shoe leather looking for an agent. I'd done a professional play when I was 17 whilst still at school as I'd been down to my local rep company.

The Artistic Director had heard that I'd given up teaching and said, "If you're interested, there's a job for you here." That was in Barrow-in-Furness where I went into weekly rep. In two years we did 96 plays. It was good training, especially for getting out of trouble when you couldn't remember lines. It was hard but I loved it. Then I went down to London and I got a job in the chorus at the Palladium. That was my first major job in London. Eventually I got a part in one episode of Z-Cars. Then it went from there: odd little bits, World of Wooster, Red Cap, Court Martial, The Saint, all sorts of bits. Then I got a lead in a television play and then I got a lead in another television series. It was only one episode of a thing called "The Villains". It was all about crooks and crooks were the leading characters. Then I got into Doctor Who by accident really.

I played a character called Morton Dill. The Tardis arrives with the original Doctor Who, William Hartnell, and his team shortly afterwards pursued by the Daleks in their time machine. I had a 10-minute sequence. It was really very funny. Immediately after, I was offered a part in the show and I did 46 episodes. Only 17 episodes of mine exist now.

I'd been an actor 10 years by that time. After Doctor Who, there was very little work around then. I did about three different episodes of Z-Cars and different books and a few odd tiny bits but no work to mention, really. I drove trucks, did all sorts of stuff. Then, out of the blue, Blue Peter asked me to go and audition.

They'd been told about me by Giles Havergal, a director I'd only met once. He happened to be at a dinner party where a woman told him that she'd heard at a previous dinner party about a week earlier that Blue Peter were looking for someone to take over from Christopher Trace. I got the job. It's as simple as that, really. Serendipity - right place, right time.

They interviewed me three times. I was a lifeguard, I was a really good swimmer so that was how they introduced me to the programme.I was teaching John Noakes and Valerie Singleton about life-saving at Crystal Palace baths and at the end of the program, we all are in the pool and he looked at the camera and said, "See you on Monday." That was why I was suddenly in the show.

I was brought in as the balance to John because he didn't learn scripts very well and he wasn't very good at remembering factual stuff. The programme needed someone who could carry that off.

I did a lot of stunts myself as part of the show – I did the famous one with the Furniture van. The vehicle I was supposed to be driving didn't have any safety equipment in it. There wasn't even a seat-belt when I got there. They put one in and I went, "Okay," and gave it an experimental tug, and it came out of the floor. They had to put something else in, and it eventually seemed secure.

I used to rock climb, I think I did four films with Chris Bonnington climbing in the Lake District.

We also did a film about rescuing an injured airman from the top of the crag. We had to climb the crag to get him down. That was quite exciting. But I liked all that.

5

Hilary: How did they decide who did what stunts?

Just random, though Jonny was earmarked for more. I was never asked to do parachuting. I'd love to have done that. I did a lot of the driving stuff, so racing cars and speed way; we did all sorts of things. Of course you do it with virtually no training. You meet somebody there who gives you about 5 minutes of instructions and then you just do it.

Hilary: Any lasting injuries from any of it?

I don't think so. I've had to have a new hip. I don't think that was due to any falls I did, no. That was just my stupidity in later life as I fell off a roof and broke my heels. That wasn't very bright. I fell 20 feet and people die from that. I was in a wheelchair for three months and had to learn to walk again. I didn't work for a year so yes, that was a difficult time. As far as filming was concerned, I nearly cut my foot off in Fiji when we were laying some railway tracks! I had about 12 stitches in my ankle and an awful lot of blood. My foot turned red.

Hilary: How much time did you get off you before you were filming again?

That was the last film we did in Fiji. We flew to Tonga and I was laid up for two days and then we had a Sunday off. We went out on a boat to a lovely coral island which was really quite small.

You could walk round the whole island on the beach in about 30 minutes. It was a beautiful island. Then I decided I was going to put my foot in the water. This was dangerous because coral can be quite poisonous to a cut but anyway, it healed my ankle. I was walking again after that so I was able to do the other films.

Shaun: What was the budget like when you went on expeditions?

Lord knows. It wasn't very much. Didn't pay us much- about fifteen pounds a day. That's all. They weren't generous to us.

We stayed in nice places. We were going to stay out in the deserts in Morocco in a sheikh's tent but he didn't turn up. We ended up in a reasonable hotel but it had been requisitioned by the army. Some of us slept in offices on sofas for a couple of nights and then we got rooms. But normally the accommodation was okay.

I can't remember us being in dreadful deprivation. You stayed where tourists would stay. In Ceylon we stayed in rest-houses, which had sparse and basic accommodation, but it was comfortable. Just got to check that you haven't got a scorpion under your mat or a snake or something else. Accommodation was always all right.

Shaun: How was Biddy Baxter to work for? (Editor of Blue Peter)

She was responsible for the show. I think she's responsible for the fact that the show has run for 60 years. She was very dictatorial. She was a total control freak and I must say I didn't get on with her very well. I had as little contact as I could with her which meant I rarely went into the office.

On studio days she was all right, but she had some weird ideas. She'd change the running order of the show with 15 minutes to go before you're on air. It's a live show: about 6 cameras, vision mixer, lighting guys, all the rest. Then the whole order of the show is suddenly changed - plus us having to work out where we were in the script

Luckily we were good at our job. We had to be. She wasn't easy to work with. I had a few run ins with her but I stayed there for 10 and a half years so it couldn't have been all bad.

Shaun: Did becoming a presenter give you new challenges?

Yes, It took me a while to learn to be myself! I was about six months into the show before I felt comfortable every time. I think to be honest that it was probably six months longer than that before the producers were comfortable. I think it took them longer to be happy with me than I took to be happy with myself.

The first few months were quite difficult and I'd get told you're being "schoolmaster-ish" when doing things. So yes, I had to lose all that.

Hilary: How did you get the job presenting Crufts? (a famous dog show)

Because I had looked after the programme's first pet dog, Petra, I did many of the dog related items on the show. After Crufts we would always have the Obedience Champions and the Best in Show in the studio, and I would commentate on what they had done. So when I left the show in 1978, I was asked to introduce Agility to the TV audience at Crufts. And it went on from there. I have now been Presenter and commentator at the show (for TV) for 40 years.

Shaun: Did Petra have any idiosyncrasies?

She wasn't the ideal dog to have around children. She was a very poorly puppy. She had distemper as a puppy so when her second teeth came through they were all

very spongy. She didn't have any front teeth which I think was just as well around children. She didn't like the studio and when I took her over to live with me (which I did from about 1968), she became a happier dog, but she never really

liked the studio. She wouldn't mind being near me, but she didn't like other dogs.

She came from a pet shop in South London. It's not surprising she wasn't a very good dog, but she loved me. She was 15 when she died, which was a good age for a dog.

Shaun: What was Percy Thrower like? Was he as eccentric as he seemed on TV?

I think we used to get on very well. I don't remember ever having a cross word. I was quite bored with the gardening items after a while though. He was a very pleasant man with a rich Shropshire accent.

Shaun: Besides the elephant episode, can you think of anything that went really badly wrong but you managed to cover for it?

Not a lot, because the show was so highly produced. I can remember we were doing a film about demolishing a high chimney in South London. They set the charges and we helped them. Bang! But it stayed up! Then it became very, very dangerous. Who was going to go in there to see what it was? It could have fallen. We didn't stick around for the final demolition.

Then we had the Girl Guides and Brownies singing a song around the camp fire which actually caught fire in the studio. The firemen had to go in and pull it out. We were on air so that was live.

When I was rock climbing, we had a few scary moments. I can remember being stuck at one point. I got up beyond this sloping wall onto the straight wall and climbed round and I couldn't find a hand grip. It was a difficult corner to get around and behind me on the other side was the camera man, the wonderful Mick Burke - he'd climbed up on his own, and he'd got a camera which was quite heavy and a bag of film and he's free climbing with no ropes!

He was saying "Reach a bit to your left Pete! Up a bit." He was there and he was filming it hanging on and guiding me. I eventually found the small handhold, swung myself around and got across the gap.

Shaun: At Blue Peter, did you mix outside of work?

I mixed quite a bit with Johnny; not a lot but if we were away filming then yes. We were away filming quite a lot and, of course, we always had nearly a month away during the summer expeditions and we spent a lot of time together. We were very different. He was much more reserved I suppose than I was. He was quite a shy man, but we were very close friends..

Shaun: Was there any real rivalry between yourself and the competing TV show, Magpie?

Not from us individually. There was obviously rivalry between their programme and ours because we were after the same material. Our Monday show screwed up their Tuesday and their Friday show screwed up our Monday if they were showing the same things, and vice versa.

They were doing their job and we were doing our job. They were slightly more trendy, I think, than we were. but in spite of that we're still getting the same audience essentially. It did split the audience I'm sure. But we were still getting eight and a half million viewers so our audience never suffered.

Shaun: Have you got any regrets about your career at all?

I only took the job on Blue Peter for six months- at least that's what I thought. When the contract ended, I discovered I didn't have the option and that they had the option so I signed for another six months. By then I liked it much more so didn't want to go and leave it but I did not want to be a television presenter. I wanted to be an actor; I wanted to make movies throughout and I never gave myself really the chance. When I left Blue Peter, the BBC gave me a load of work. They gave me Stopwatch which I did for five series which was a sports program for kids. I did We are going places, which was holiday ideas for kids' days out. And there was Kickstart, Junior Kickstart, and all of the BBC Darts coverage for eight years.

Shaun: Were there any big parts offered to you when you were in Blue Peter, but you were contractually obliged to turn down?

I was never offered anything. I may have been, but the Blue Peter office would've handled it and they didn't ever pass anything onto me. I was never invited by the office to open Fetes or to do personal appearances. I honestly believe that there was an element of blocking my career because they stopped me doing things. It annoys me; it's not a regret, but it's an annoyance. They wanted the control. I'm angry about it. No, I'm not… not anymore. But the contract we signed was very restrictive. The BBC owned our careers!

My regret would be that I didn't make movies, I really wanted to.

Shaun: The rise of reality TV stars, how do you see that?

I wouldn't call anyone who's appeared on reality TV a star.

That irritates me immensely. If people have been on television for five minutes they think they're stars. It's horses for courses. The audiences like it. I've never seen an episode of Love Island. I've seen two episodes of Big Brother. I've only seen a couple of episodes of "Get Me Out of Here I'm a lunatic". I have no interest in it, let's put it that way. Actually that's not quite true. I actually do like Masterchef. I quite like that but if I never saw it again I wouldn't mind.

Shaun: After Blue Peter?

I've commentated on Darts events, Crufts obviously! And many other sporting events.

I also ran a Video Production Company for 13 years in the '80's and 90's. and have presented many big "live" events and hosted many arenas at Country Shows, including a ten year stint at the Royal Show at Stoneleigh in Warwickshire. I directed pantomimes for years. I Did 30 major pantomimes up and down the country with lots of the big stars: The Grumbleweeds, Cannon and Ball, the Chuckle Brothers. I've got quite an impressive CV in that department.

John and I went into pantomime as soon as we left Blue Peter. We did pantomime that Christmas and we worked together as a double act for seven years. I started directing the second year, then the third year. Mainly because our director didn't turn up for the first rehearsal, so I said, "Come on, let's get this show on the road." That was it.

CRACKERJACK!

Crackerjack was an unsophisticated show – it was daft… It was funny in a corny sort of way… It was just the sort of show that appealed to me when I was about 5 or 6 years old – full of sketches and skits – one moment they were parodying another TV show, and the next they were doing a ventriloquist act (none of the actors were actual ventriloquists mind you!) – But that was the fun – it was meant to look frantic, and thrown together – that was the excitement… And even when I was growing older, I still liked to dip in now and again…

FROM LAS VEGAS Live ON STAGE

BERNIE CLIFTON

Bernie was at the Heart of Crackerjack during the early years that I watched it, along with Peter Glaze, and he seemed to be the one having most of the fun! His props were often home-made, and whilst everything looked thrown together on the show, there was a definite warmth emanating from the crew. But Bernie stood out for me, and he would be a regular on TV for many years, popping up unexpectedly in the oddest of places!

Where did you grow up and what was your childhood like?

St. Helens. We were poor, and we lived in a terraced house. All the kids in the area wore clogs. Because we'd no idea that there was any other form of life, we were happy.

I was four when they dropped a bomb on the street which landed three doors up from our house. It just missed us by about 20 yards. Somebody was looking after us that night.

I didn't enjoy school too much. I was not the best student, although I passed my 11+ by some kind of fluke and then got myself into Grammar school which was a total disaster from year one to year four. Instead of going through for the GCEs and the A-Levels, I just left under a cloud at the age of 15.

My first job was like the Hovis lad – I was delivering bread for the local Co-Op and then I ended up as a plumber for St. Helens Corporation. I didn't have any sort of aptitude for that kind of work, but it didn't seem to matter as long as you had a trade as the man said.

At the end of that, I did two years National Service in the RAF, again as a plumber. I then found myself as a radar mechanic. We were deployed at the RAF bombing school in Lindholme in South Yorkshire, which was on the doorstep of South Yorkshire clubland of course. I found myself singing at weekends. That's the talent I had then, working in and around the clubs and doing very nicely thank you. It was a learning curve.

Were your family entertainers?

Not at all. I came from St. Helens of course, and nobody from there seemed to be involved in show business. In fact, when I announced my intention of giving up plumbing and staying in Doncaster and doing the clubs and the pubs, it was generally agreed by the family that I was "going to the Devil". I must have really upset them. Fortunately, my parents lived long enough to see me have some kind of success. But during that period there was a lot of headshaking going on.

How did you get into the prop side of comedy?

I think coming from St. Helens, in Merseyside, we had a lot of Irish in our community that worked on the building sites. There was this kind of anarchy - A lot of the tradesmen had been in World War II. They'd come back with a certain attitude, a certain sense of humour. We'd do anything. Practical jokes were the norm and there was actually a kind of bubble of mischief, I suppose, that I had grown up with. Finding myself on stage as a singer, there always seemed to be several props there left by others. I sometimes incorporate these into the act.

I was singing a bit and doing a few gags, and this led to a role on "The Good Old Days" which was being filmed in Leeds. Les Dawson was topping the bill. He must have seen something in me because he took me to one side and said "You're okay doing that, what you've done tonight, but you're like one of a hundred just like you. Why don't you find a style?" He said, "What do you really enjoy?" I said, "Well I love mucking about with props." He said, "Well why don't you go out and be a prop comic, a visual comic?"

I took him at his word! Within a year to two, I had accrued this mountain of props, such as a joke mike stand. Which I used to fill up with marbles and then I'd put it on its stand and then the first thing I did after my opening song, I just picked the mike stand up leaving the base behind and this avalanche of marbles would go down the stage. I had to plan it because you didn't want people slipping on the marbles after the show – so I used to go into a club early and fix a gutter down the front of the stage so that the marbles would run down-hill to the front and go in this gutter and then fall into a biscuit tin at one end. You'd have this cacophony of sound!

Were there any comedians that you really liked, and did you base yourself on anyone?

Ken Dodd at the time was my number one and then people like Tommy Cooper. In the film world, the Marx Brothers. I loved that kind of nonsense. There was always a surrealism about the places that these kinds of comedians could take you to which was distinct from the patter comics. I was always attracted and leaned towards that other dimension of comedy, the visuality and it's never left me.

Were you in a situation ever in a club where your act completely bombed?

How long have you got? All the time. It's that thing about when you were only there for a reason and you were just filling in between bingo and whatever else the clubs had planned. The north of England wasn't a very forgiving place. There's that old saying: "If they liked you, they let you live'.

Any kind of pit village would have at least one Miners' Welfare club, a couple of social clubs, perhaps an Ex-Servicemen's club and a pub or two that did entertainment. They were tough because they were seeing entertainers maybe three, four, or five nights a week. I was lucky in a way, that as time progressed, I was now delivering full-on comedy. I was trying it out, but I'd got my singing voice to fall back on. I really admire the comics who walked in with nothing but gags. It was only during that period that the props started to turn up in my act and it was initially a difficult transition.

You were on 'The Good Old Days' but how did you get the transition to the other shows like Crackerjack and so on?

Well, it was a slow process to begin with. Working the clubs and establishing a reputation was first. I started doing Summer seasons in the late 60s and early 70s. I did two or three of them in Jersey. Then I got a role on the Lulu series in the mid-70s doing a 13-week Saturday night show as the comic, which was unbelievable exposure and led to me getting the job on Crackerjack.

Did you have to tone your act down for shows such as Crackerjack?

No. It's interesting that if you look at night-club entertainment now, it's adult humour. I'd be doing midnight in cabaret clubs all over the country and it was more family orientated humour, even at that late hour. You could entertain families and you would be accepted doing that form of wholesome family entertainment.

Crackerjack was filmed live, wasn't it?

Virtually. I think it was a 50-minute show. The recording time we were allowed was less than an hour. We were told particularly by our producer "If you make a mistake, it will go out. We won't stop." and that literally was the case. It was a great learning curve. You were out there, and the kids were screaming, you were doing sketches, you were doing songs and either props wouldn't arrive, or the prop wouldn't work! Or somebody would do something wrong. You sort of powered through it.

Back when we were doing it, we were doing three sketches and then finishing with a musical finale featuring parodies on all the pop songs that you could insert. We'd maybe do a Napoleon sketch and we'd manage to get a laugh. It was wonderfully creative. A special time.

What was the social life like in Crackerjack? Did you all socialize together?

Not particularly. I was a Northern lad and used to commute up and down as much as I could. I was doing the clubs again at weekends. Peter Glaze lived down in Kent, so he would commute. Ed Stewart lived locally. We all kind of did our own thing. When we went in, I think we had a five-day turnaround. We'd get the script on the first day and we'd hammer it, change it, scrap

it, burn it, or start again and by about the third day, we just about got it. Then it was almost time for the dress rehearsal and then the actual show. It was pretty hard work. The first thing I'd do when we got to that two-day break was either jump into my car and head off to the south to do cabaret or I'd head up to Derbyshire and have time with the family.

How did you persuade Oswald to buddy up with you?

Ah Oswald the Ostrich! He's retired now incidentally! Well, by the time I got to the mid-70s I got a pair of biscuit tins. I was dancing then I got a big lion costume to wear to dance in and then I was doing a ventriloquist act with a cat on my shoulder.

I had been to Shepperton film studios to one of their auctions and I'd bid for a 12 feet long rubber shark. I also had a guy at that time who was making my props. He was called Peter. He'd done the cat thing for me and some other stuff for my act that I was working on. I just had the idea to have the Ostrich costume, and Peter said, "Oh good, I think I can do something with this." He rang me a few months later and said, "Do you want to come and try it on?" I just went down and said, "Oh, yes." And I liked it. Having said that, it took years and years for it to get to its current look. I think we perfected it in the end, but the initial one was pretty crude and basic, and I think it was only by spending a lot of time and money on improving it that we got it to its current stage.

London Marathons?

Yes, I watched the first London marathon in 1981 and there was a father and son, and they completed the first marathon in a rhinoceros costume. The father was bent double at the back. And I suddenly thought, you know, if they can do that, I bet I can do it on the Ostrich! I'd got the Oswald the Ostrich as part of my act by this time, I found myself on the start line of the marathon in 1982.

Having trained like a commando for six months, I still didn't think I'd complete it. I thought I'd get halfway around and then just call it a day, but I finished it! I think it was about four hours 15 minutes which is remarkable.

Subsequently, I did it every year, I did it for six years until on the last one I did - I ran out of steam at the half way point - and they had to wrap me up in some bagging foil to stop me from dying. I was just doing what appealed to me, and, as a result, it was things like the marathon that you just remembered. It's like the path that you take, the journey, we're not getting too profound, but it just follows it indefinitely or just following your nose.

Do you ever think that you could have made it as a straight up singer?

Absolutely, that is my ambition now! I always say that I was a singer that got in with the wrong crowd… All I ever wanted to do was to be a singer with a dance band - even though I was having fun with the props and the comedy, I really was an out to out singer. I've just met up with this singing teacher in Sheffield, I've heard about him for years and years and finally got together with him. He's made such a difference. I go every week and I work out vocally every day.

Why did you audition on the TV talent show "The Voice"?

I sent off an audition for The Voice without telling anyone. I didn't tell my family. I didn't tell my agent because if I had, they'd have tried to talk me out of it. Eventually, there I was, auditioning for "The Voice" posing as a "retired plumber from St. Helens", a 79-year-old - and fortunately, got through all the different processes until the "blind audition" right at the very end. This is where they face away from you and judge you solely on your voice – and if they like you, they then spin around in their chairs. They didn't turn around though – but even though they didn't turn around, it made such a difference. People went, "Wow." That's then they revealed who I really was of course, when they spun round in their chairs – It was especially funny for Ricky Wilson (one of the judges on 'The Voice') because he'd had this experience with me as a child. His father took him to a show that I was performing on. I came out on Oswald the Ostrich and frightened him to death. He was only six. To quote Ricky: "It defined his childhood".

What's that thing about not meeting your heroes?

But that appearance on the show directly led to me working as part of a show, singing in Las Vegas! It reminded people that I was still kicking around, and that I could actually sing.

What do you think about reality TV shows?

The pendulum has swung too far, hasn't it? Well, it's easy, isn't it? Turn the camera round and watch people. We're watching people doing everyday things now, aren't we? I don't know if there's a cure or an antidote for it. But things always evolve, don't they? Things will change again.

Last week I went to see "The League of Gentlemen" TV show, on tour, in Buxton. Absolutely amazing. It's like seeing a superstar rock band. They've got articulated lorries and scene changes and a big tour coach, with blacked out windows. A big double-decker! They're doing arenas.

When you think of what it was 20 odd years ago you couldn't possibly have imagined that, could you? That you'd be watching comedy in arenas and stadiums?

Were there any opportunities or role that you missed out on, that you regret?

It's twists and turns, isn't it? I've auditioned and gone up for shows. I'd fail but perfect the audition in the car on the way home, usually. Too numerous to mention. At the end of the day, it's my story though, isn't it?

It is a business. Regrets? Yes. I suppose I would do a few things differently. Every life is a unique story, isn't it? It's a journey. I do sleep at night though. We're only here once. And it is never too late, whatever you've got, give it a chance to flourish.

Play School

Play School is one of my very first memories of TV. Back in those days, children's television had "proper" adult presenters who seemed more like the best teachers at school rather than the over-enthusiastic twenty-year-olds who dominate that type of programme now.

It was based around learning and playing at the same time, and often songs and the toys (Humpty, Hamble, Big Ted and Little Ted) would be dragged along to take part.

There was nothing sophisticated about the show. The toys just sat there, and the presenters did all of the talking and singing obviously. But there was something comforting about the show with its lack of pretentions. I think I really did get to know that "The wheels on the bus went around and round" by watching people sitting in a cardboard box with paper plates stuck on the sides.

Presenters on Play School in the era rotated regularly too – You had Brian Cant of course, Cloe Ashcroft, Floella Benjamin, Toni Arthur, Fred Harris, and of course Johnny Ball….

Johnny Ball

Johnny Ball was my favorite presenter on the show. The others were great but there was something about his eyes – sort of twinkly and mischievous. He later scripted and performed the Science and Mathematics series "Think of a Number" and the many off-shoots.

You started out as a Butlin's red coat didn't you? Did you always want to be an entertainer?

Yes, I did, but I went into the forces when I was 18 and signed on for three years because I wanted to get a full experience. If you signed on for three years at that time, you got a choice of your career path and that was great. That was my University in many respects.

When I came out I could have gone into air traffic control from my experiences in the RAF, but, at the end of the day, I knew what I was going to do and I went straight to Butlin's. I applied and became a Red Coat – I spent three years with them and, again, this was a valuable education.

Were your family entertainers too?

My Dad probably would have been a comedian if he'd ever got the chance. It probably never occurred to him to try, and so he never had the chance really. He was an iron founder all his life,

but when he met my friends, other comedians, they would say 'He's funnier than you isn't he?" and they were right! He was wonderfully funny. That's where I got my desire to be an entertainer from. I also got my desire to learn about science from my Dad because he was very open-minded and he used to always have an interest in the latest developments in science. I loved maths from the beginning though, because my Dad taught me lots of maths tricks playing 5's and 3's at dominoes, with the double 9 game. My Dad always said other versions of dominoes such as double 7, double 6 dominoes were just for wimps. They were a great teaching aid for me when I was only about 4 or 5 and I am looking at the set we used to play with now across the room and that was 70 to 76 years ago.

You went from Butlin's as an entertainer to the club scene – that must have been terrifying?

Like every new gig it can be quite scary but they were mostly wonderful. There was an agent called Mike Hughes who got in contact and we made a deal. I started working for him as soon as I left Butlin's around 1962.

I started doing Saturdays and Sundays in working men's clubs and I slowly built up my act. You had to have two or three variations depending upon the needs of the clubs and the length of time on stage. I had my "core" act and just varied it and then turned "pro" in around 1964.

How did that lead to the TV work?

By '67 I'd already been earmarked by a lot of people to appear on TV. Back then you had a compere when a band was playing live. I'd already done tours with The Rolling Stones

and Dusty Springfield so my name was getting known. It was hard work because no-one could hear a single word you were saying as there were lots of screaming kids!

That's where it all started. My act began to develop in the clubs with taking on a few more aspects and I thought I was strong enough to actually be on television. I genuinely think I was one of the better club comedians at that time so it was only natural that

eventually people would start looking at me for television. Eventually I got an offer but not one I was expecting really!

The BBC got in touch, and they wanted to see if I was interested in working with BBC children's television. Now at the time, this wasn't as outrageous as it sounds as a lot of the comedians coming through the club scene were going straight into light entertainment and even children's shows. We weren't blue; we were just entertainers. This was particularly true of Northern comics coming from the general Manchester area and North West in particular for some reason.

So we thought it would be for CrackerJack. I went to the interview and it seemed to go well.

I thought I'd got it within three minutes but then he said

'You're going to be great on Play School'. I said 'What?' he said 'On BBC 2 at 11 o'clock in the morning' I said 'Oh, I'm not interested!" and I tried to walk out!

He got me to come back and he got me to do the audition. First of all, I wasn't very good because I didn't want to do it. It wasn't something I was expecting to do so it was a bit awkward but then I realised the integrity of the people

making the show. So, suddenly, I thought 'I can learn television from here can't I?"

I joined Play School and I actually stayed 16 years in the end so obviously I was doing something right. Whilst I was there, I could do anything else I wanted. I would have a couple of months off where I was doing other things and then I'd come back and do more Play School. So, it was lovely in that respect because it paid quite well and cushioned me and allowed me to spread my wings a bit into other areas.

At the same time as I was signed up to do Play School, I also got the ITV Christmas Night Spectacular which was an hour and a half show. That was recorded in late November for Christmas night. Burt Flanagan was on the show. I was the last person to ever do a double act with Burt Flanagan on television, because he died a few months later. It was a star-studded bill and I was a very mild sort of compere.

After that my agent also got me an interview to go onto the Val Doonican show as a comedian. I managed to get that and I went straight into that the following week.

Something else happened around that time that would change my career for the better. I knew a neighbourhood friend of mine was into science and technology and I used to go to meetings at the Royal Society with his group. He said 'You're a natural, you shouldn't be doing comedy you should be doing science and mathematics'. So that's where it started.

The BBC had noticed that I was doing quite a lot of the writing on shows. I wrote the comedy parts on "Play Away", and they must have thought "Right, we'd better

get him his own show to write". So, they asked me what would I do if I had my own show and I said 'I'd probably do a program on maths.' To my amazement, they let me do it. That show became 'Think of a Number', which was the first time I'd created a format and turned it into a show from scratch. I didn't know what I was doing really, but the first series we won a BAFTA and we were away. My director, Albert Barber, and I just dovetailed. I would say what I wanted to do and while I was saying it he would draw the set and we'd get planning. I wrote the scripts for every show.

On Play School what was the filming like? Was it quite hectic?

You film two a day. You do five in two and a half days. You'd record them and, because of the nature of the programme, they were soon being repeated. In fact, they were the first program shown in colour on British TV purely by accident - colour should have started the night before but there was a BBC strike. Because we were the first program to go out in the morning at 11 o'clock, Play School became the first one

in colour. Then they repeated it at 4 o'clock in the afternoon. So we were well paid because every time you did it, you did five shows with five repeats and the repeats were paid at 75% of the original fee so it was a sensible thing to do from a financial point of view. The calibre of people like Derek Griffiths did it too.

Did you find it difficult to have to learn scripts on any of your shows? Particularly Play School, which had a very fast "turn around" filming wise?

No, it was alright. For Play School, frankly, I could look at the script and I knew it. You get so good at it you just don't have to think and it just goes in. I've got a good retentive memory. So I had no trouble at all; I could do it almost effortlessly really. The 'Think of a Number' shows and the 'Think Again' shows were different because I wrote them and as I rehearsed them, I strengthened them and changed them where needed as we went. We made programs about 35 minutes long but our spot was 27 minutes so we had to squeeze it by cutting out any waffle and keeping it really firm. It was great.

Did you get offered any roles in adult television?

Yes, "Tomorrow's World" asked me if I would join as a presenter (following in Fred Harris's footsteps of course), but I'd gotten the writing bug then, and so I said 'Can I write my own show, my own pieces?' They said 'No, you'll have a writer'. I said 'But I've just written 20 series of television programs' and they said 'But you're a good presenter' and I said 'Could it be I'm a good presenter because I have had good scripts?' So I turned them down three times.

I couldn't transfer to adult television. But that was alright because by the late eighties/ early nineties, the corporate world was beating a path to my door so I worked for National Grid for 6 years, British Gas 3 years, BAE systems 4 years doing lectures and things like that. I wasn't full time; I would do several weeks a year with National Grid. It was only about 8 days a year but they were very intense days and they paid me a lot of money. I won the sales video of the year award.

I was out of television now and BBC children's television had collapsed; it was no longer what it had been and I didn't want to be part of it so I walked away and I worked for Central. I didn't like that very much and didn't have enough control so I walked away from that too.

So about 93' I wrote a stage musical, 'The Michael Farraday all electric road show' and that toured for 3 years with National Grid subsidising it. I still had the bug so I wrote another one called 'Let the Force be with you' which went very well and then again in 2000 I wrote 'Tales of Mathmagicians'.

Do you ever think you missed your calling – would you have wanted to become a teacher?

No because I wouldn't like having the same audience twice. If I had to do the same set of children all the time it would very difficult. Also the curriculum is far too narrow at any one time and it drives me mad.

I do lots of conferences and I don't talk about the curriculum. I talk about where I think the kids should be, and what they should be teaching them at this age. There was a piece in "The Times" recently and it compared maths exams between the ones for kids in the 70s and 80s and the maths exam for the "millennials" and it's far easier today. The reason for that is that it's taught slower and they can't fit as much into the curriculum. You don't get people enthusiastic about it because it's taught slower and people lose interest.

So, as a by-product, we're producing less scientists and less mathematicians really or at least not very good quality ones, so it's not good at the moment.

Rainbow

Rainbow
was a children's TV show, that was a strange mixture
of Sitcom and Puppet theatre. It featured an overly colourful house
full of cardboard furniture and painted on windows.

Geoffrey (played by Geoffrey Hayes) was the single dad, with a family that included a 6ft tall
talking bear, a pink hippo and Zippy (no one is completely sure what zippy actually was) ...

Geoffrey was the sensible, kind parent, that wasn't shy of
telling off the "children" if needed. Bungle was the happy
go lucky one that frankly wasn't that bright, and seemed
permanently perplexed, George was the sensitive one
that was easily hurt, and Zippy was the sarcastic
nasty one, prone to temper tantrums, and was a
bit of a know-it-all. Out of all of them, Zippy was (I
think) the one character that most of the children
watching the show identified with the most.

Ronnie le
Drew was the leading puppeteer
on Rainbow for most of its existence,
operating both Zippy and Bungle, as well as
having a long and distinguished external
career in films and other TV shows.

Ronnie le Drew

I was fond of puppet shows as I child, and have a lot of fond memories of shows such as Rainbow. Why did the Independent Television companies start making their own pre-school programs when they already had Sesame Street from America?

When we had Sesame Street. on Channel 4. for a while, The independent companies, after talking to educationalists, said, "It's too Americanised. The spellings are all wrong, and some of the pronunciations are not right. You should make your own programmes." Basically, companies like Thames, Yorkshire, and ATV all got their heads together and decided to make their own pre-school programmes. One of the early ones was Rainbow then Pipkins started on ATV. Various companies decided to do their own shows. In my childhood there was Sooty, and Muffin the Mule, not forgetting the puppets on Watch with Mother.

The very first image that appeared on British television was a dummy's head. So, the history of mannequins and puppets goes back a long way in broadcasting. It's in our psyche to like puppets because as kids liked having cuddly toys to talk to - telling them our private thoughts. They were safe to confide in, and in many ways', puppets are similar to that. Being small like a child, a child can identify more with a puppet than an adult.

As a child I did actually have some puppets. I lived in a council flat in South London. There wasn't a lot of money, but we did have long summer holidays. In those holidays, my sister and I got together and put on shows. Now, these were probably not very good, but the local kids in the flats would come along and just sit and

watch because we all had a lot of time to spare then.

I had a wind-up gramophone player and some dreadful old records. I had about three puppets made by Pelham Puppets. They were marionettes, they were fairly expensive to buy, but I managed to get hold of some and did shows. I had a few glove puppets too. I was doing puppets in a daft, amateur way, but I managed to get good reactions from the kids.

While I was at senior school, which I didn't stay at for very long to be honest, my only friend who was interested in acting, drama or theatre, got an audition for the musical, Oliver, which was way back in about 1961,. He said, "Well, come along with me," so I went along with him. There were loads of kids. They had all read the advert in the Daily Mirror; "Wanted: Workhouse boys for new musical."

So, my friend sang. and got the part of one of the workhouse boys because he wasn't too tall; I think he was just over four foot-something. I was about 4'8", so I was just too tall. I was terribly disappointed. Back at the drama club at school the bigger lads said to me "We don't want this puny little kid in our drama club. Two rejections, but I still had my puppets and thought I can be any sort of character if I do it with a puppet." I could be a lion or a mouse and nobody would know as I would be hidden from view. my own body would not be an issue.

All I had to do was change my voice according to what puppet I was working. Puppets were becoming very important in my life. I did find that there was an organisation called The British Puppet and Model Theatre Guild. It had its meetings not far from where I lived, a short bus ride and I was at the meeting where I met up

with fellow enthusiasts. They were husband and wife teams mostly who were performing their own shows. They had wonderful marionettes, ones I'd never seen before, and worked much better than mine did.

At one of the meetings I met John Blundall. He made the puppets, for instance, for Thunderbirds, he designed Parker (Lady Penelope's Butler) from that series . I'd been watching all of those Gerry Anderson shows on TV like so many kids did of my generation Torchy, Four Feather falls, Supercar, and Fireball XL5.

I was terribly excited to meet him. He gave me a photograph of the Fireball XL5 puppets which I took to school and showed off and said, "Look what I've got" you lot will never have this!" I was getting my own back on them, showing off my prized possession. Anyway, that, in a way, started me thinking that I wanted a career in puppets. I didn't know how I was going to do it, as I was still in school.

John Blundall took me to the Educational Puppetry Association (now defunct) , I met a wonderful puppeteer called AR Philpott, but known in the puppetry world as Pantopuck. He did perform his own puppet shows, but concentrated on writing and education, a wonderful teacher and mentor, He thought I had got a talent, and he let me play with his puppets and his stage. I thought this was fantastic. His wife was a lady called Violet. She made me a couple of puppets, and

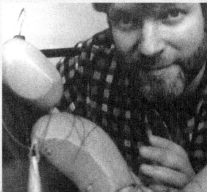

then I started to make my own. I was never really a maker before because I always thought making puppets wasn't my forte. I thought I could charm my way in getting people to help me make them - and was mostly successful.

I made a stage and did shows for children's parties. I had also written to Bob Pelham of Pelham Puppets in Marlborough, Wiltshire. He wrote back and said, "There's a puppet theatre called the Little Angel Theatre. You might be interested in going there. They might offer you a job?" I wrote to the BBC. They said, "No, we have all the puppeteers we need at the BBC. We think you ought to go to Art school first. We don't have any vacancies."

When Bob Pelham gave me the address of The Little Angel Theatre, I went to the Puppet Guild. They said, "Yes, it's just opened. We're all going, Sadly, there wasn't room for me on the coach. An Australian puppeteer called Edith Murray was visiting the country and said. "Look, I'll take you. I know John Wright. We can introduce you, and you can see the show" how wonderful is that I thought!

To cut a long story short, that's when I started. I left school at 15. I didn't stay for exams, and I joined the Little Angel Theatre after writing a letter to John Wright. I was their second apprentice. I worked there for six months with no pay, then I got £2 a week. Now this was about 1963-'64. The pound was worth a little bit more money then. My father was a teacher and we weren't earning megabucks, but they supported me with fares from Stockwell to the Angel. My eyes really widened. Being in a theatre, they had the most wonderful Marionettes. They also made and used glove puppets, shadow puppets, and

rod puppets all these were used in the theatres productions, The company still produces new and exciting work for the public to see.

Believe it or not, I'm still involved in the Little Angel now after all these years. well over 50 years now. It's extraordinary. I'm now what they call an Honorary Associate along with Lyndie Wright, who was the founder director's wife. I'm a board member, and I'm one of the performers in their Christmas show. It's been an amazing time, really.

I was there for eight months to begin with, and then I went on to work with a puppeteer called Jan Bussell who was famous for the Hogarth Puppets. He was the puppeteer who started Muffin the Mule, the very first television puppet icon in 1946. Obviously, I wasn't around at that time, but I did work for him in the '60s, which was a wonderful experience. Then I was given the television job on Rainbow. John Thirtle, the puppeteer who had taken over from, Violet Philpott, (a mentor for us both) sadly injured her back and had to retire from the show. John Thirtle took over, and then he retired after a bit because he was setting up a show called Playboard for the BBC with his partner

He was a brilliant puppeteer. Sadly, he's no longer with us. He was a wonderful maker and very intelligent. He made puppets for Playboard, then he went on to make a series called Button Moon. which his partner Ian Allen wrote. He couldn't carry on doing Rainbow, so he phoned me up as I was a friend and asked if I would take over Zippy?"

It was amazing because just before the beginning of Rainbow, the producer and a researcher came to visit the Little Angel Theatre. I suppose they thought they would

get some ideas for puppets from our puppet theatre. At the time, and I always think this is a bit of a coincidence, I was having some puppets made for a children's show that we were going to do for their Saturday morning shows. One of the puppets had a great big zip across his mouth. It didn't look like Zippy, but it had a zip for its mouth; I still have the puppet.. It's a brown potato shape thing. My idea was that the puppet would talk too much so they'd zip him up. They were wandering around looking at stuff in the workshop and I'm sure the researcher saw this puppet with a zip across its mouth.

Then suddenly around 1972, there was Rainbow and a puppet with a zip for his mouth. I thought, "What a coincidence." I always like to think that maybe they saw my puppet at my theatre. and thought they would have a puppet with a zip! Who knows...?

I carried on with Rainbow up until it finished. when Thames TV lost their franchise. The history of the programme was this, it had been on for a year and they'd had various changes. The original Zippy looked a little bit different. John Thirtle, being a brilliant maker, redesigned Zippy and now it is the puppet that everyone recognizes. He also made the George character because George wasn't in the original series. They thought it would be nice to have a foil for Zippy, George was born and he became the perfect foil.

They have got a new voice man. I didn't actually do the voice of Zippy at the beginning. A man called Roy Skelton did the voices for many years. I took over when, for instance, we went to open fetes or did charity things. Roy lived in Brighton and he had family, so he found it difficult to go up to London to just to voice the puppets and sit behind a wall. If it was a fete, you just have to hide behind something. It was easier for Jeffrey and the singers to be there because they're just there as actors and that was fine. With the puppets, it was always trickier.

So, I took over doing the voice for Zippy. I did some of the live events. I was copying Roy's voice, really. Sadly a few years ago, Roy died. I was asked by Fremantle Television, who owned Thames, to take over and do Zippy in various appearances, and I'm still doing appearances with Zippy now. Just last year I did the programme for Channel 4 called The Last Leg, live political comedy satire.

They asked if Zippy could appear because one of the presenters said that they had had a tweet from one of the viewers that said, "You sound like Zippy from Rainbow." The guy said, "No, I don't!" so they thought it'd be a funny idea to surprise everybody by Zippy popping up the next week. So, I popped up and they loved it; the audience went mad. I did a full skit where I pretended to be him as Zippy and introduced a few items.

I've done Children in Need. I did a thing for a charity just two weeks ago in Margate where Zippy and George appeared. It was for a young person's' cancer charity. They just thought Zippy and George would be great to appear and open it and say, "What wonderful jobs you're all doing!"

Fremantle Television or Fremantle Media own the brand. Every now and again, they ring up and say, "Can you do this? Can you do that?" It's still carrying on, even though it must be over 10 years since it finished on screen but there are DVDs. They make huge amounts of merchandise even now and it's still selling, so they're quite happy. Sadly, it's not

something that I get any money from but that's fair enough. I'm just an employee and it's been amazing journey through the years.

When you work on, let's say, Rainbow, how do you coordinate your movements to the speech? You must get a copy of the script?

Yes. I'll give you a breakdown of how we did the programmes. We'd started the week on a Friday morning or afternoon with a read-through. We'd record three programmes a week. We'd get three new scripts. The writer who wrote masses of scripts for us in the early days, a man called John Kershaw, would get them to us. I think he wrote a few hundred scripts.

We'd read through with the producer, the director of the programme and the cast. The production manager would time the read-through to make sure that the scripts fitted the time. Originally, the programs were just under 20 minutes. Obviously, with independent companies, they've got to be absolutely to the time so that they can get their commercials in.

Then the producer and the PA would go away, leaving us with the director, and we'd what we call "block" the moves. We'd have two chairs representing where the window was, then we'd have a table and we'd put two chairs behind. We didn't have any monitors to see what our puppets look like. We just had to be there with it. They'd read through and say, "This is where I want you to stand. Geoffrey - you do this bit. Bungle, you're going to stand over there and you'll come through the door there".

We didn't have a mock-up of the set. We just had a tape on the floor just like actors do in a rehearsal room.

On Friday afternoon when we finished about lunchtime, we'd all go home and we'd all supposedly learn our lines. I did learn them a little bit so that I would know when Roy was going to speak because I'm stuck under a table behind the window or whatever. I found that I got to a stage where I didn't actually need to learn the lines because I would get to know when Roy would take a breath. He was sitting in the studio in what we called "Roy's hole". It was quite funny. He had a soundboard round him, and a monitor so he could see the show and the puppets. He could also look above the board and see the live action if he wanted, but cameras would be in the way a bit. He'd got a monitor and he'd obviously have the script marked out for George and Zippy, and so he would obviously do the two voices which was amazing.

After the weekend, we'd go back on the Monday to the rehearsal room in Teddington Yacht Club. It sounds very grand, but it wasn't really. We'd go through the moves again without the script this time because, obviously, they would have learnt their lines, apart from Roy who was reading. Over the weekend, Geoffrey might have made a few changes to the script, just to make it easier for him. Same with Bungle and Roy. Roy might say, "Actually, I don't think it's a very good line- could we try that line?". Then we'd go through it say two or three times, and then we would go back home again.

On the Tuesday, the producer and the PA would come in, and we would present the three programmes to them- lines learned, moves learned, and they would time them. If, for instance, we'd extended the timing a bit, we'd have to do some cuts. Then everything was ready to go to the studio the next day on the Wednesday.

Wednesday was quite a long day. I eventually went on to work on a few series. I used to go by train originally because I didn't have money for a car. Once I had done a few series, I could afford to drive in. Usually, I'd have breakfast in the studio because there were lots of programmes going on and they had a canteen. I think we'd start between half-past eight and quarter to nine, and that would be a camera rehearsal in Studio Three which was the smallest studio in Teddington Studios. It's sadly no longer there now; it's all been knocked down to make luxury flats.

We would do all three programmes so that the director could then point the cameras to make sure that the camera script was working properly, and we were happy with what we could see.

Also, for the first time for us, we had a monitor, a little television screen, because, as puppeteers, we are hidden under the table so that was the only way we could see it. We'd watch the puppets and their reactions; We'd see the same pictures as the directors. We'd see all the cuts so that we could get the puppets looking in the right direction. Obviously, they had to look alive and focused.

Roy had the same thing. He could look at the monitor and see how the whole thing was shaping. In a way, that was our best way of rehearsing as far as we were concerned. We were under the right tables. We were sitting in the right low chairs that hid our heads from showing.

We did two programmes on a Wednesday. Quite a busy day and I didn't get home usually till about 8:30 at night because I lived in Islington by then. It was quite a job to travel from Teddington to Islington and we wouldn't finish until usually around 7:00.

On the Thursday, we just did one programme. The musicians always wrote a different song for every programme. It was amazing really. Sometimes their numbers were quite complicated. If it was a complicated number, we might do two songs on that day so that they could have more time to get that worked out properly. It all depends on how complicated the programmes were. That was something the director worked out with all the camera guys, the props people and the scenes people. And that's how the program was made.

Originally, they were very educational, but we got a bit more fun in with stuff like "Zipman and Bobbin" and taking the mickey out of "Batman and Robin."; just going out to space and all sorts of wonderful things.

Originally, we did about 26 weeks a year of Rainbow. It was quite a long time and there weren't that many other companies doing pre-school programmes. We also got an award. In those days it was from BAFTA, but it wasn't like the BAFTA children's award they have now. It was a children's award called the Harlequin.

Was it quite uncomfortable a lot of the time?

Some of the time it was, We were very lucky as we had little wheels under our chairs, so we could move around a little bit. As puppeteers, we would find ways of trying to make it a bit more

comfortable. For instance, there'd be shots when it was a closeup of Geoffrey. We could just relax our arms a little bit then because we knew when the next shot would be (because of the camera rehearsals.) we'd be ready.

I've done other puppet things on television where it's been much more uncomfortable. The sets were built too short. We were standing, and I was having to crouch to get my head out of shot when I was walking a puppet along a corridor.. With Zippy, I used to put my head into the bottom part of his costume so that you couldn't see my head appearing. The bottom of the puppet didn't conceal my eyes, so I could see the monitor. The table was probably the most uncomfortable. They built a counter on the other side of the opposite side of the window, which was a bit higher. That was quite nice because we could move around a little bit. We also had a garden scene where the wall was covering us.

It was funny really because we were on these low trolleys, and we were using our feet to go along. If we were standing, obviously we could move a bit easier, but that wasn't the case. It wasn't really until The Muppet Show started that the puppeteers could stand for them. They could get extra movement because they had a big studio and a lot more money to put into the programme.

It just depended on where we'd had to be, and if any scenes were too long then it could become very uncomfortable, but luckily The scenes were fairly short, so it wasn't too bad. Bungle had a head that came off. He'd get terribly hot wearing that skin running around and doing stuff. There'd be breaks for him to have a bit of air.

In the camera rehearsal, he didn't put the whole skin on. He just put on the head, which was quite wide, and wore gloves, so to get a two shot for camera shooting, he just played as an actor. He didn't put the full costume on until the actual takes. It would be quite funny to see just the head and gloves of Bungle and a short man underneath. It was easier for him, in a sense and it still helped the cameras to get the shots right too

The Bungle suits and the actual puppets, how did you clean them?

The Bungle costume could be sent to dry cleaners, but the puppets couldn't, sadly. We actually had several sets made over the years. Pamela Lonsdale, the original producer, would say, "The puppets are getting a little bit grubby." Zippy was made out of towelling so any bit of dust would get onto his costume, and very quickly he would look grubby. George was not so bad as his costume was a different material.

The mitts we would wear for paws would get dirty because you'd be picking up things because we did all sorts of funny stuff like chucking things and holding real food. Sometimes they all got sticky and very messy..

Bungle's head couldn't be dry cleaned. He had what we called "Bungle's tutu" inside the suit to make him look really fat, and the actor also wore a gauzy thing that it made him much fatter and gave him the plumpness we needed. If he'd just put the outer skin his body, it would just hang very straight and look no good. The tutu was always dry-cleaned after every Thursday, so it was fresh for him for the next performance.

Do you think Zippy was misunderstood as a character?

Misunderstood? I think the kids understood him completely. They adored him because he got away with all the things that they couldn't get away with. Things like being slightly selfish, being very 'know-all", and basically being very demanding. As a kid, you think, "I'd love to…" You would start saying that and then your parents would say. "No, you can't do that- don't be horrible." If he got too much, of course, the lovely thing was that he was zipped up. All his vocal tirades were put away like that. He had to pat his mouth to say, "Mm-mm-mm. Let me out."

Of course, Geoffrey was being the father figure. He would say "Look, you behave, and then I'll unzip you," That worked really well. I think George, again, was the perfect foil. He was this very shy, quiet friend so Zippy could dominate him.

Funny enough, as the series went on, George changed over

the years a little bit. We had several different scriptwriters. The actual cast were offered the chance to write the scripts, so Geoffrey wrote some of these. Freddy Marks, who was one of the singers, wrote some scripts. Roy Skelton (voice man) and Stanley Bates (who played Bungle for many years), wrote scripts, they knew the characters' words. We all knew the characters so well by then. We'd been doing it for many years and so they really got to grips with this, and they became really strong characters. Roy would write something for George and make him not exactly "bolshy", but a bit stronger, and sometimes he'd get his own way. I think writing our own scripts developed the series. More and more people fell in love with it.

I didn't really know how much the series meant to people until we finished doing the programmes and we started doing student union gigs. And the fans would queue around the block to see their favourite characters. And soon Fremantlemedia started producing masses of Rainbow T-shirts, and then DVDs came out, followed by mugs, purses, and bags. We did an update of the Rainbow theme and released it as a single. Suddenly we were on Top of the Pops and we got up to 13 in the pop charts!

What was it like working on the show? Did you all socialise, and were you friends outside the show?

We did to a certain extent but not that much. We were so busy. By the time I was halfway through doing Rainbow, I got married, had children, and I felt that I wanted to get back home quickly just to see the family really, so I didn't stay in the bar afterwards, but some of the people lived nearer. Roy had a family as well. Rod, Jane and Freddy - They'd stay around and have a drink, sometimes, with the director of the programme but I tended to go home. We remained all good friends. It's amazing really. We had our disagreements like, "Oh, I don't think Zippy would say that." "Oh yes, he would." "Oh Geoffrey, get that right." if anyone did anything wrong It wasn't taken personally; we all got on really well, we still do. I didn't see Geoffrey very often, but we did have a meet up a few years ago.

Occasionally, I see Jane at social events with Freddy - they're together now. I did see Geoffrey at that point and I hadn't seen him for ages, but every now and again we get together if we hear that a director has died. Sadly, when Roy died, I couldn't go to his funeral. I was working at the time, but everybody else went along. And sadly this year Geoffrey and Pamela Lonsdale have gone now too.

How did the film work come about?

The film work came about really in the breaks between Rainbow. Jim Henson had done a film called The Dark Crystal, over at Elstree Studios. Then he put out auditions for a new film called Labyrinth, so I said, "This will be great." It was perfect timing, so I went along. A friend made me a little puppet, and I did an improv with it and sure enough I got the job, working as an extra puppeteer in Labyrinth, and from there, we were put on a list of puppeteers because Jim loved working in England. He thought the technicians were brilliant. I think originally, they only wanted about 20 extra puppeteers but in fact they used 40. It was my first major film that I'd worked on. It was amazing.

We did goblins and various creatures, but it was wonderful experience. My Next film was Little

Shop of Horrors. It was Frank Oz who auditioned us for that. I did bits of the plant, the leaves and the tentacle things that were coming out. Then I did Muppet Christmas Carol, and then Muppet Treasure Island.

We weren't the main core of puppeteers as the Americans were doing the main characters. We would help with an extra arm for a character or we'd be other pirates, in Treasure Island. And more films were to follow but until they are released I can say nothing.

There's a Rainbow episode that's infamous. It's quite rude?

I know the one you mean! We made it in 1976? It was for the VTR people. Obviously, people make mistakes; they'll swear or something like that say, "Sorry. Shit." Then they cut that. They sometimes kept those blooper tapes. Programmes have been made since about bloopers. Both BBC and the Independent companies collected the outtakes and showed them to their company at Christmas parties - ITV companies had a competition for the best bloopers and they said, "What about Rainbow doing something?" We were told by our producer that we were certainly not going to swear and carry on inappropriately, but we could do a programme. We all got together one lunchtime - it was a Thursday because we had time free at the end. We actually recorded it in the studio. We had Zippy saying, "One skin, two skin, three skin." So not quite saying "foreskin." Then we had Jane playing with her "knockers" and Geoffrey "playing with his balls". It was all that schoolboy humour. If you played it to a young person, they'd think it was just a normal Rainbow. The

children wouldn't know. Of course, we adults certainly knew what we were doing and how we kept a straight face doing that I don't know, but we did it. As it was Rainbow, we always said goodbye at the end of it all and then of course we all screamed with laughter afterwards. by the way we won the competition this all happened in 1976.

Somebody had got a copy of it and it was played on Channel Four on one of those late-night programmes and that started people thinking, "Oh my God, this is hilarious. All the Rainbow characters are being a bit naughty." Then of course when YouTube started, it was out! It was not supposed to be recorded. It wasn't meant for public consumption. Nothing is sacred anymore nowadays.

Is there any puppet job that you always wanted to get but never got?

I don't think there really is. The only thing I haven't done is worked puppets in a Circus Ring in a circus. I've done nightclubs, and school disco type things. I've done things that I'd never have thought I'd do. I've trod the boards, working in some amazing theatres and productions worked in TV and Film. Teach my craft and enjoy life what could be better!

THE WOMBLES

"The Wombles" was a TV show, that used stop-frame animation to portray lots of little rat-like things that ambled around on Wimbledon Common, clearing up rubbish, and having adventures. Most of these clothes wearing things (voiced by the legendary Bernard Cribbins) avoided humans at all costs, and spent their lives inventing new ways to keep the world tidy.

Then all of a sudden, they were appearing on Top of the Pops – bashing out great Pop-Rock!

The band (created by Mike Batt, who would later go on to create other hits such as the theme from Watership Down - "Bright Eyes") had hits with "Remember you're a Womble!"

Chris Spedding

Chris Spedding played lead guitar on a number of "Wombles" records, and has also played with Roxy Music, Sharks, Tom Waits, Roger Daltry, and Jeff Wayne amongst others.

What made you want to become a musician?

Well I grew up near Sheffield, and as far back as I can remember I wanted to be in a band. My parents weren't supportive of it though, and tried to steer me towards classical music – they even had me playing the violin. I wanted to switch to guitar once I heard skiffle music and rock music for the first time. Eventually my parents gave up and sent me to a classical guitar teacher, and that really developed my playing skills and taught me how to score music too which came in very handy later on. But I learnt to play a lot of music just by listening to records. I moved to London in the 1960s – I suppose the biggest influence then was a group called Mike Berry and The Cruisers that were local to me.

By the time Mike Batt came calling to ask you about becoming a Womble, you had already built up a fantastic CV – what was your first reaction, and how did he try to sell the idea to you?

That's not how it works at all. I was a freelance session musician. I got a phone call from Mike and

I showed up with my guitar. Mike was one of many who employed my services previously, and I'd worked for him on many projects before he started making the Wombles records. We actually worked on lots of "jingles" for radio advertisements – that's how Mike started out – he had a knack of creating really catchy tunes out of nowhere, and so he was ideal to come in and do things like the title music on shows and so on.

He had a deal with the BBC – instead of getting a fee for creating the opening track for The Wombles children's show, he was given the rights to use the name "Wombles" on records. It was a great deal for him, as it meant he could create singles using the name, for a show that was already well known and established, but it was still a huge risk for him – no one had created a group like "The Wombles" before, and there was no guarantee the singles or albums would sell of course! When we recorded the Wombling Song it had no special significance for me or any of the other musicians. It was just another session. I have no particular memory of doing the session. When we make any of these records, we have no idea if they will be a hit - we never do - how can you tell?

Sometime after it was recorded, I left the session world to join my own group – Sharks, and stopped doing sessions for two years. This would be around 1972. I remember Mike calling me to try to persuade me to come and record the follow-up to the Wombling Song but I declined. So, I think maybe session guitarist Alan Parker played on the follow up record. By 1974 I was back doing sessions – Sharks had some great tunes but we didn't make it big, and by this time I knew that Mike had a new "brand" with the Wombles – as that was what it had turned into

really. The songs were all hitting the charts. I was doing record sessions for David Essex, Sweet, Typically Tropical, The Drifters and many others around this time, as well as releasing my own "Motorbikin'" song which was a big solo hit for me. But there was never any question of me "joining" or being asked to join the Wombles as it wasn't a band in the traditional sense. We were paid session fees for our work and that was the end of it.

There was a silly Musicians Union rule that you had to re-record a song for a Top of the Pops appearance. I thought this was silly because the whole premise of the show was to feature the top-selling records of the day - but the viewers never got to hear the actual records on the show, only a hurriedly put together recreation of them! Most of the session musicians hated doing this, and the producers and artistes hated it too. Most of the musicians turned down the offer to redo the records so these original musicians were rarely on the remake. But on one occasion I accepted the offer to appear with Mike on TOTP as a Womble. I thought it would be fun, and it was.

I was proud of what Mike had achieved with the Wombles. I thought his records were good and very imaginative. But there were never any musician credits on Womble albums, obviously to preserve the cute fiction that the furry creatures themselves performed everything! Fair enough! But since I was getting a lot of "ink" in the musical press for my session work with other artistes and thought I'd like some credit for the Wombles - the biggest-selling act of all my clients. So, I proudly mentioned my Wombling to a music journalist. This didn't always have the effect I desired (for instance: one of the more amusing jibes in the musical press referred to me - because of Motorbikin' - as the "leather Womble"!) So I suppose the

Womble association seemed to hurt my credibility as a "serious" musician in the minds of these pundits. But I didn't care about that because I thought my Wombling was something to be proud of. It did hurt Mike though because he continued to write great songs and make great recordings of them, only to have them ignored because his voice sounded too much like a Womble. These great songs became recognised - and were hits - only after other artists like Art Garfunkel and Katie Melua recorded them.

How did the Womble songs come together? Did you all have input?

All Mike's work. Writing, arranging, producing and singing. Mike would book the session - sometimes with a full orchestra - and we'd cut maybe 3 songs in a three-hour session. Mike was pretty meticulous – he would always make sure that he came prepared for every session as they were so expensive – so he knew exactly what everyone would be doing and when – and we were all experienced session musicians that could just come in and play pretty much anything thrown at us – so the sessions were tight, and we would try and get things completed in as little time as possible.

You are quite a shy person in real life but quite creative – the same as the character that you played in the band – Wellington. Was that a coincidence?

Yes of course – I always assumed Wellington had a bit of a naughty side, which is why I used the arrow shaped guitar!

When you were playing live you had to wear those enormous suits didn't you? Were they uncomfortable?

I only wore the suit once (on TOTP) and, of course, you didn't play in them. We mimed. Since the Womble heads didn't have mouths, lip syncing wasn't an issue! And in case you were wondering - there were no Womble suits at any of the recording sessions! It was impossible to play in the suits, but at Glastonbury some of them managed it. I appeared as "me" with no Womble suit. Also, even though we only used the suits for Top of the Pops and for "live" shows, they were very heavy and got a bit wiffy after a while, as there was no way of cleaning them. But the suits were very well made – Mike's mum actually made them! There is a story out there that Mike had to actually have a pee in his suit whilst on stage – I couldn't validate that story though!

Playing as a Womble at Glastonbury, even without the suit must have been amazing?

My only memory was that each Womble character had an understudy in case the suit got too hot and the musician inside needed a break. So far as I remember, no one took advantage of this. Not even Mike who was a total trooper throughout. The other Glastonbury memory was that Mike gave away simple cardboard Womble masks to the audience. After our set, the next big act over on the main stage was

Paul Simon. What Simon thought of hundreds of Womble faces staring up at him is not recorded. But must have been very confusing for him!

You lived on Wimbledon Common in real life when you played in The Wombles didn't you?

Yes, though in a house of course, and not in a Womble den or whatever they are called. It was something the music press picked up on and mentioned at the time.

You have played on a lot of hit records – Motor Bikin' was your big solo hit – do you prefer being the front man in a band or are you happy to be part of the background?

Being a sideman is far less stressful. But obviously everyone likes to be in the limelight every so often. I'm proud of all of my solo work – with Sharks and with Motor Bikin', and it's great to know I can write my own music. There are still a few albums in me yet!

You continue to work on some great stuff – can you imagine ever retiring?

I can't afford to retire! And I'd miss playing. There are still some great acts that I'd like to play with. I'm still waiting for Bob Dylan to call.

Children of the Stones

Children of the Stones was by far the scariest TV show I had seen as a child. The opening titles set the tone, with grotesquely misshaped stones shown at imposing camera angles, all to the sounds of eerie chanting and shrieking.

The show featured Gareth Thomas, who played astrophysicist Adam Brake and his son Matthew, who both arrive at Millbury, a town which was built in the centre of a stone circle at Avebury. Something is amiss and there seems to be a conspiracy between the town-folk and the mysterious lord of the manner, and before you know it, people are dancing around in circles and turning into a new stone circle.

The show is probably quite tame by today's standards but it traumatised an entire generation of children in the 1970s.

Jeremy Burnham

Jeremy Burnham was a well-know character actor who featured on many hit shows in the 1970s, such as The Avengers, The Saint, and Randall and Hopkirk (deceased) before turning to script-writing, and Children of the Stones is regarded as his masterpiece.

You began life as an actor – were your family quite theatrical?

Yes, a member of my family was already involved in the profession. My Aunt Barbara was a producer and director at the BBC, and, at one time, she was the highest-paid woman in both TV and radio. She also started the Salisbury Arts Theatre after the war, so when I told my father I wanted to go to drama school, he sent me down to Salisbury to do an audition for 'Babbie', as she was known. She reported to my father that I had enough talent to go ahead and recommended the Old Vic theatre School in South London, run by Glen Byam Shaw, George Devine and the great Michel St. Denis.

What was your first big break into the profession?

My first big breaks were being accepted by the Old Vic School, then being accepted by John Harrison at Nottingham Rep to play the juvenile leads for two seasons. The third was my performance in Jean Anouilh's 'Point of Departure' at Nottingham, for which I got rave notices in 'The Stage'. That attracted the attention of H.M. Tennents, at the time the most

prestigious producers in London, run by 'Binkie' Beaumont, who sent for me to do an audition for Robert Morley. He was looking for a young actor to play his son in his own play 'Hippo Dancing' which ran for fifteen months in the West End. Other West End hits followed, including 'A Passage to India' and a star-studded Tennents production of 'The Rehearsal' and another Anouilh play with Maggie Smith, Alan Badel, Robert Hardy and Phyllis Calvert.

How did your switch to screenwriting come about?

I was an actor long before I became a writer. The switch was made when I chatted to Patrick McNee while filming an episode of 'The Avengers'. I told him I'd love to try writing for the show because it was very much my cup of tea. He said they were looking for writers, and suggested that I talk to Brian Clemens, the producer. So I did: I suggested an episode set in a cold-cure clinic, with a huge nose set in the wall. Tara King would fall out of the nose, and Steed would say 'gesundheit!' That was the beginning of my writing career. I'd already

appeared in three episodes of 'The Avengers' and I wrote five more. What I didn't realize until I was invited to the fiftieth anniversary of the show at Chichester university was that I was the only person who both wrote for the show and acted in it. I was treated like a God!

Which were your own favourite film roles?

All of them, but especially 'Law and Disorder'. That was an Ealing comedy with Michael Redgrave and Robert Morley. I also liked 'Bonjour Tristesse', playing Jean Seberg's Parisian boyfriend in Otto Preminger's production with David Niven and Deborah Kerr.

Children of the Stones scared the hell out of me as a child – where did the idea come from? Were either of you interested in the paranormal or stone circles? Was there any pressure to make the series more "child-friendly?"

Neither Trevor Ray nor I can remember where the idea came from, but we had worked together on

'Paul Temple' and we lived close to each other in North London, so we used to meet for coffee and discuss various dramatic possibilities, out of which came an idea that we both knew was a winner. Neither of us was particularly interested in stone circles or the paranormal: we just knew it had to be really scary and we were right. The reaction from HTV and Peter Graham Scott, the director, was exactly what we had hoped for. He said, "This story is for children??" If we'd made it 'child-friendly', as you put it, it wouldn't have worked and that was why we asked for equally scary music.

Were you involved with the music side of the production?

No but there is an interesting story connected to it – The producer, Peter Scott was driving past Avebury late one night with the radio on and scared himself to death. A classical piece was playing by Polish composer, Krzysztof Penderecki, and the combination of the circle in the distance, and the twilight, along with the music chilled him to the bone, so he suggested that we use something

similar in this in a children's show! The production team got in touch with Sid Sager, and he put together an acapella piece using the Ambrosian Singers who were a leading choral group from London. The Singers had worked with lots of famous singers and feature on many of the big feature film scores from the 1960s onwards. A repeated Icelandic word was used throughout "Hadave"; chosen because it sounds spooky. We don't know what it actually means. It probably means "sandwich" or something like that!

Do you think that the production team did a good job?

I think they did a marvellous Job! It was

a very expensive series to make. They even had to make a few fibreglass models of the stones to fill in a few gaps in places. Veronica, my wife, played a part in the series, and she said that you would often get Japanese tourists that would watch filming. They looked open mouthed when the film crew picked some of the stones up after shooting a scene and drove off with them! I think the location and the quality of the actors and actresses were all top-notch!

How do you think the TV show was received?

It is generally regarded as the scariest TV show for children ever and I think it made a huge impression on quite a lot of people's childhoods. Maybe not for the right reasons though!

THE TOMORROW PEOPL

The Tomorrow People was a science fiction show set on Earth, and followed the adventures of the next step in Human Evolution – Homo Novis, and their mentors "The Tomorrow People".

Children born to normal human parents were beginning to "Break out" and show supernatural abilities, such as Telekinesis, Telepathy, and Teleportation. Along with "TIM" their computer, The Tomorrow People were a sort of early version of "The X-Men" – the team's job is to locate others of their kind, to keep them safe – and to train them to wield their powers accurately and responsibly for a common good. It also had one of the creepiest sound-tracks I've ever heard, along with an obviously "Twilight Zone" inspired introduction. It could be a little bit lame in places, but there was enough invention and action to keep everyone hooked.

Nicholas Young

Nicholas Young was an already successful character actor, appearing in shows such as "Upstairs Downstairs" and prestigious TV plays. He played "John" in The Tomorrow People – the Lynch-pin of the team.

You started quite young when you were acting. What sparked the initial idea to go into acting?

I was inspired specifically by Walt Disney's film "The Prince and The Pauper", which I saw in my school holidays in 1962, and I was instantly hooked. It starred a young Australian actor, Sean Scully. He played a dual role in the film, and I was really fascinated by it. I went back to see it three more times before it came off a couple of days later by which time, I had the entire script in my head. I thought, "This is what I want to do." I could literally recreate it word for word for word. It was quite extraordinary.

We all have our obsessions. It might be a place or a film, or anything else when you're that sort of age. I wasn't terribly good academically and nagged my parents to send me to a stage school instead of the planned public school. My grandfather had been an actor, so my father was in a bit of a weak position to say no. I managed to clinch the deal by failing my Common Entrance exam for public school, not once but twice. In the end they gave way and allowed me to go to a place called the Corona Stage School which, in its day, was quite well respected and produced a lot of well-known stars of the day: Susan George, Judy Geeson, Richard O'Sullivan, Dennis Waterman, Francesca Annis, and so the list goes on. That's where I went when I was 14.

I spent half the day concentrating on academic studies and the other half was vocational. In other words, singing, dancing and acting. The school had an agency attached to it so by the time I was 14, I had starred in a film called Eagle Rock; the first colour

production made for the Children's Film Foundation in 1964. It turned up on a channel called "Talking Pictures TV" recently. I had to speak with a Welsh accent for the film because I was supposed to be from Wales. I even had to deliver a few lines in Welsh!

Did you find, being a child actor, that the other children around you who weren't actors treated you badly? – Did you come across any jealousy?

No, I think the good thing about the school I went to is that you're growing up with children who are in exactly the position you are. No-one can bully or put you down because you're all doing the same thing. Some of the friends outside acting would say, "I wish I was doing that instead of studying for my GCEs," but there was no unpleasantness about it at all. People quite liked the idea. I was able to be self-sufficient. I used to collect military medals and I was lucky enough to buy a rare one in a junk shop for a pound which I then sold on for £350. I was soon earning enough money as an actor to pay the school fees and my parents couldn't complain. I worked fairly regularly so I thought at the time, even though my parents might have wished otherwise, I was probably going to make a go of it, so it was okay.

In those days there were a lot of one- off plays that BBC and ITV used to make and I appeared in a lot of those with some really top actors of the day. People like Michael Horden, Ian McKellen, Ian Carmichael and Patricia Routledge, I did one or two television series that have long since faded from people's memory. There was the one called "Front Page Story" in which I played a young aristocrat and then something called "The Flying Swan" which was supposed to be an inn run by Margaret Lockwood who was a huge star in those

days. She starred in the film "The Wicked Lady" and many others.

Did you find acting quite easy?

Yes. I didn't have any difficulty with that. When you're young, it's easier to learn your lines because your brain is receptive but when you get older it's more difficult. I perhaps didn't appreciate at the time that I was working with some very fine actors. I suppose you retrospectively realise what great actors they were. It was a great privilege to work with those sorts of people and you would pick up an awful lot of tips. Not one of them was difficult to work with. They were all very welcoming, very helpful and very friendly.

Obviously, The Tomorrow People is the one that we identify you with the most. How did the role come about, and did you have to screen test for it?

Yes, the other one I did before "The Tomorrow People" was "Upstairs, Downstairs." That was a very popular series in its day as well. Again, playing the same sort of role - I specialised in playing snotty, sneering public schoolboys. Although I'd never been to public school, I learnt to play someone who had. I think I got the maid pregnant in "Upstairs, Downstairs". That was great fun (the role – not getting her pregnant!). It was shot in black and white simply because, even though we had colour by then, the ITV technicians decided to go on strike because they claimed there was more work involved in shooting in colour. It was total nonsense of course. They hung on to the show for six months before they brought it out. Funnily enough, because black and white gives people a sense of a period rather more than colour does, it didn't spoil it one bit. In later years it was left off the DVDs because people had become used to colour by then and expected it.

So "The Tomorrow People." happened when I was helping out my agent in her office; and in the early Seventies, we got a request from Thames Television from a casting director saying, "We're doing this programme. Have you got any suitable young actors?" I was given the job of collecting all the photographs and CVs of the various people who we were going to submit and obviously I made sure that mine was on the top of the pile. That in itself didn't get me the job as I had to go and audition for it. I met Paul Bernard who was the first director. He was a former "Doctor Who" director so he knew how to do science fiction. I met Roger Price, the writer, and Ruth Boswell, the producer, in Euston Road where Thames TV had a presence in those days. I had to read the script and Roger Price said that I wasn't how he had envisaged John, but when he saw me play it, he thought, "Yes, this could work quite well".

You've got to bear in mind that this was in the early '70s, and his idea of including the ethnic mix was, if not unique, then extremely unusual. That, I think, contributed to its major overseas appeal. It was sold to 55 territories and it was truly an international cast. It was also not class conscious particularly. You've got John at one end, and you've got Tyson at the other, and

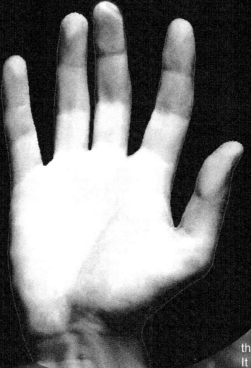

everything in between. It appealed to all children, at all different levels, which was very clever.

Doctor Who was sort of a rival, at the time. There seemed to be a lot of friendly rivalry going on?

Maybe. I thought "The Tomorrow People" was better than "Doctor Who". Now, that sounds pretty arrogant to modern ears because "Doctor Who" is so beautifully made nowadays. It's faultless and it's an excellent programme. You have to bear in mind that in the 1970s, it was rubbish. The sets wobbled, and the Daleks couldn't even go up and down the stairs; it was just a joke. I think it was bad on many levels and although "The Tomorrow People" was also pretty bad in all those respects, it was certainly

a perfectly good rival to "Doctor Who". Dr Who was broadcast on a Saturday or Sunday afternoon at about five o'clock, so it was a children's programme with a young adult mix as well. "The Tomorrow People" was aimed at people who were entering adolescence. Everybody I've spoken to who loved the programme, said that they felt empowered by it because they felt maybe they'd been picked on or bullied at school, and they were finding the transition from child to adult very difficult.

This whole concept of someone breaking out and developing all these special powers triggered the imaginations of a lot of children. That element was missing in the American version because the actors were that much older. It was beautifully photographed, produced, directed, acted, and everything else, but the concept was probably not quite right.

What did you think of the idea of The Tomorrow People, initially? Did you have any interest in science fiction at all before then?

Well, I had an interest in science, and how the universe was created, and I still do, but I can't honestly say that I was a sci-fi enthusiast. I was brought up in the '50s and early '60s when sci-fi things and special effects were rubbish, and it was almost a joke. It just wasn't as sophisticated as it is now. Even though it's science fiction, there are rules in science fiction, which are every bit as immovable as science fact. You can't just sit down and write any old rubbish. It has to be plausible as far as the fans are concerned. I have to be honest that it was a difficult decision to know whether to go into a children's programme for more than one series because I was doing other good quality work. I didn't know when I started that it was going to go on for years. Then, when I came out at the end of it, all I had to show for it was seven or eight years of children's television. Producers don't tend to treat children's TV actors with very much respect, unfortunately.

Did you have any problems with props that malfunctioned?

No, the main problem was with industrial action in the '70s, when Britain was suffering from a dreadful disease; when the unions had the country by the nuts. Out of the 70 odd episodes we shot, about three quarters of them had to be reshot because the unions were being so difficult all the time. I remember once that I tried to move one of the chairs which was in my way, and they threatened to strike. I was hauled over the coals because they said that that's a job for a technician, not for an actor. It made life very difficult in that respect. We could've done a lot better than we did, but I think low budgets had a lot to do with that. I'll give you an example. There

were quite a few scenes where we were supposed to be floating in hyperspace. This was achieved by having us suspended in a

harness, but you could see the wires! I'm a bit of a perfectionist, and I said to the director, "This is ridiculous, we look like something from "Thunderbirds"."

We did most of our special effects using a technique called chroma key. It's now called green screen or blue screen; but the screens used with chroma key were yellow in colour. People stood in front of a plain screen, much the same as they do now, and the background was super-imposed electronically. The camera was set to ignore the colour yellow so I said, "Why don't you paint the wires yellow, then they won't show up?" It just hadn't occurred to anybody in there. The

director said, "We haven't got time to do that." One of the technicians then suggested that we could put some yellow gaffer tape round the wires and it worked; it was perfect. With a bit of care, I always felt that we could've done a lot better than we did.

You once said you thought the sets were better and more sophisticated than the Doctor Who ones by far.

Yes, I think that's right. I wasn't being so arrogant as to suggest we should be considered better than "Doctor Who"; I just meant that, at that time in television history, we were better. I know people joke about the model space craft made out of tea cups. I think it was me that actually pointed that out, but I think it was a rather good use of a plastic tea cups, the ribbed parts of which look like an aluminium if you paint it them silver. With care, you can make all those things look reasonable.

You became a bit of the pin up, with the success of the show. Was that quite a strange experience?

At the risk of sounding conceited, no, I didn't find it so. Even though we'd gone through the kitchen sink phase and there were working class heroes around, I think people still expected their leading actors to be reasonably good looking, attractive, and fashionable. I think I realised that that was part of the job.

People's concept of good looking in the '70 was more Peter Vaughan-Clarke than me. People fell into two camps; they either loved me or they loved him (and more loved him!).

What was the social life like behind the scenes of the show? Did you all socialise together, or did you just turn up to work, and then leave?

No, we all got on tremendously well. We all had a lot of fun making the programme, and I'm still a friend of Peter Vaughan Clarke to this day. You don't see so much of my work these days, but I certainly see a lot of Peter's. He now works as a lighting rigger, and he's always in the West End, so we often have a coffee, keep in touch, and have a good laugh.

We like taking the piss out of everything. There's a sort of

mock rivalry between us about how many close-ups we'd had, and he certainly had more than I did. He was younger and better looking. We found out that we were born exactly 10 years apart on the same day: June the 11th.

Towards the end of the show, because there were financial problems across the board for Thames TV, it looked like the budget was getting reduced every year. Was that the case?

Well, I can't really comment from a personal point of view, so I can only tell you what I've heard from other sources. The main problem was the unions. The endless reshoots, which were costing Thames a great deal of money. If you look at some of the episodes, you can see my sideburns were an inch shorter three seconds later than they had been in the previous shot simply because, due to industrial action, the scenes had been recorded some months apart.

I think ultimate demise of the show was more due to Roger, the writer, finding it difficult to come up with new stories. He farmed some later episodes out to a different writer but it wasn't very satisfactory; and the final series was only six episodes. I believe there was a fire at Thames where the set got burned which certainly would have affected their willingness to make another series.

It had probably come to the end of its natural life after 66 episodes. Nowadays, that sounds like nothing, but in those days, you had to wait a whole week for your next episode so the series was spread over someone's entire adolescence. It was on for about seven years including repeats.

After the show, you were in quite a few other productions?

Yes, I think that was while I was still doing the "Tomorrow People". I get letters from people to this day about that. Someone sent me some photographs from Space 1999, while I was working on the "Tomorrow People" but it was a still from "'1999" they wanted me to autograph! I did the series "Kessler" after that and then I made a reasonable job doing bits and pieces. I did "Cymbeline" for the BBC in the early 80s and I was the only person in the cast who wasn't really a top-notch star name. It was star-studded from start to finish. I think I got to the point where I thought that this was probably going to be as good as it gets. I didn't know if I was going to be satisfied with that for the rest of my days or if I wanted to try and run a business that would bring me in a decent income. That's what made me, in the end, decide that I would do something else.

I've always been a realist. The problem was that I was playing a character in the "Tomorrow People" that was probably about 18 or 19 years old and I was still playing that when I was 28. I hadn't been able to mature into playing leading actor roles in my early 30s. I looked like I was in my early twenties, but if you put me next to a twenty year-old, I wouldn't have got away with it. My voice and physique hadn't developed sufficiently. I think I realised my limitations, but I didn't intend to give up. I started an agency that specialised in television commercials, so I could carry on with my acting career. The problem with that was that the agency did very well. I had people on the books who wanted all-around representation and once you start representing actors, you can't really be pushing yourself for parts.

It just wasn't right being an actor and an agent at the same time. Regretfully, after about five years of running the agency, I decided I would have to hang up my acting hat. I occasionally got calls from desperate casting directors saying an actor hadn't turned up so could I nip down and do this, that,or the other, which I would do; but essentially the career was wrapped up in 1981.

I did my final film appearance as just an actor in "The Great Question". It was shot in Iraq. It is a splendid dinner party talking-point when I start the conversation with "When I was in Baghdad…" because there aren't many people who can say that they've actually lived and worked there.

It was a film produced by Saddam Hussein's government. They were at war with Iran at the time, and they wanted to inspire the troops; so they made this film about some tiny little skirmish in the desert against the British in 1920. There was no set budget; it was just a case of "How much money do you need? Just keep asking and we'll keep giving". It went on for over a year but I was out there for about six weeks.

That must've been absolutely crazy. Did you have to screen test for that as well?

That's a good question. I knew the casting director very well, and she kept pushing for me. I really can't remember whether I did a screen test for that. I think it was probably just done on a photograph and her say-so. They were looking for people that they considered looked typically British. All the British soldiers had moustaches and all the Arab heroes had beards. It was a great experience. All the other actors moaned about the place,

but I said, "What else would you be doing?" I think we were being paid about £1000 a week. It was an awful lot of money in those days and we were staying in the only five-star hotel in Baghdad.

Was it a propaganda film?

It was, but it was made as a proper feature film. I've never seen it because it was never released in England, but it was a major production with all the finest British technicians and a superb British cast: Sir John Gielgud, Edward Fox and Oliver Reed to name a few. If you tried to watch it now, it'd be you might find it rather tedious. It was propaganda in the same way that Henry V, starring Lawrence Olivier, was made as a propaganda film during the Second World War.

What do you think of this new trend towards reality TV?

I think it's dreadful. It's often a way of making things on the cheap. Much of it is self-financing. They're not using professional actors and it's turning people's brains to mush. There's room for every type of television but television companies simply will not produce the sort of plays I was talking about earlier on because they don't want to spend the money on one-off productions. When they do a drama nowadays, it's usually a mini-series made as a co-production with three or four other companies because no single company has got the budget to make it on its own. The reason for this is that you don't get 20 million people tuning in on one evening to watch the show anymore because the audience is split across so many channels – and so, therefore, is the advertising revenue.

People said to me when multi-channel television first came out, "Oh, this is great!" I said, "It's not. I've seen this in America. I know exactly how it works. It's the same 'cake' divided by a hundred channels. There'll be no money, no budgets to make decent television, and everything will become cheap and tacky," which is exactly what's happened in the short term. Fortunately co-production has allowed for bigger budgets and there is now some excellent television out there; beautifully produced and well-acted.

Is it true that you were in Beadles About?

Yes, I did about 40 of those. That was after I became an agent. Again, I got to know all the casting directors; Nikki Finch was the casting director concerned, and she called me in to do just one episode. The whole point of it was that the person who was setting up the gag didn't feature heavily; it would be self-defeating if everybody got to know what you looked like.You wouldn't be able to fool people if they recognised you from earlier episodes.

It did need somebody who could think on their feet and improvise well. I did one or two and then it sort of developed from there. It began when Nikki told me that she needed an actor who was a pilot. The gag they were going to play was that someone would be going for their first flying lesson; the plane would take off having "accidentally" left the instructor behind. I wasn't particularly happy about it and I said, "It's an awfully sick joke because the man's wife will probably have a heart attack."

How did the American version of The Tomorrow People come about?

They made an American series in 2013 so and I went out and did a couple of episodes. They made 22 episodes in total I think

It was produced by Greg Berlanti who made a lot of science fiction TV for America. I hadn't really heard of him but he's a well-known producer for the CW Network. I heard he was doing the show so I dropped him a line and suggested that it would be rather fun, if I made a small appearance rather like Alfred Hitchcock did in his own movies. I suggested there could be a scene where people would be sitting in a bar and John from the original Tomorrow People walked past. I didn't hear a word from Greg but then I suddenly got a call from a casting director saying they would like to test me for the show. Greg sent me a script and asked me to test for the voice of Tim because Philip Gilbert, who played the role on the original series, was by then dead.

I learned the words and we recorded it. I didn't have any notes as to whether they wanted me to play it British, American, Canadian, or whatever so I did it three or four different ways. I didn't hear another word until about four months later when I got a call saying, "Can you get on the plane next week?" My wife and I had already booked a holiday to the Canary Islands, so I sent my son (who is also Nicholas Young) in my place. I asked if we could record the role by phone as it was just Tim's voice but then Greg said, "No, it's not

just Tim. We thought it was waste just having your voice, so we've written a part for you." It was the part of an English professor working at Princeton University. They filmed it in Canada, so I flew over to Vancouver and did a couple of episodes as Professor Aldous Crick. He was a professor who knew something about the science of teleportation which the American Secret Services wanted to use it for military purposes. They were pursuing us the Tomorrow People with a view to destroying them was what it was all about. I was shot dead in the second episode and I joked that I could not therefore return in a future series. The writer said, "This is science fiction, Nick, anything is possible!"

What are you doing nowadays? Are you happy?

I carried on running the agency. I've cut down because I'm not getting any younger. My business partner died just before the American version of "The Tomorrow People" was filmed actually. I only have a small list now and I'm quite happy with that because it's a lot less demanding. Over the past four years I've taken time to write a book on the history of vehicle registration numbers in the UK. It sounds a bit geeky but actually it's a detailed social history of Edwardian motorists and contains over 800 illustrations of cars ancient and modern. I'm pleased to say It has been very well received by motoring organisations and members of the public alike, and is selling well.

IT AIN'T HALF HOT MUM

Melvyn Hayes

Melvyn Hayes seemed to form a large part of my childhood – not only was he a key performer in It ain't half hot mum, but he was also in a show called "The Double Deckers" and appeared with Cliff Richard in "Summer Holiday" – An untrained actor who brought a lot of warmth and charisma to every role that he took...

I was around 8 years old when I first started to watch "It Ain't Half Hot Mum!" – it really appealed to me – the mixture of the characters was perfect. We had the sarcastic, and often sadistic Sergeant Major (Superbly played by Windsor Davies), with his fantastic one-liners "Oh dear, how sad, never mind..." who constantly mocked the physically inferior members of his unit:

Amongst them, we had the put upon intellectual, 'La-De-Dah' Gunner 'Paderewski' Jonathan Graham (John Clegg), who was constantly scorned about his education...

The short tubby guy – Gunner 'Lofty' Harold Horace Herbert Willy Sugden (Don Estelle), who was the butt of many of the jokes...

And arguably the star of the show – Bombardier "Gloria" Beaumont – The sensitive one that tried his best to be a good soldier but had ambitions to be a big star performer when he left the army.

Each of these characters, and the others in the show all represented something that we could all identify with – even the Sergeant – a cruel man, but one with a failing career who craved glory in action but was instead stuck with a bunch of useless soldiers in the middle of nowhere.

In short, it was a superb comedy, but one that was a beautifully crafted object lesson in characterisation.

How did you first start out? Were you roped into acting as a child actor?

I bought a newspaper, The Daily Mirror, and an ad said, 'Boy wanted, to disappear twice nightly doing the Indian Rope Trick for the Comedy Theatre, London for the Christmas season' and so I phoned up and they said the auditions are tomorrow. Now the only thing I was ever good at in my Grammar School was Latin and climbing ropes in the gym, so I applied. I was the only one who could stay up the rope long enough for the London Press to take pictures, so I got the job! The wages were four pounds a week. So yes, I was almost literally "roped into acting".

For four weeks I disappeared twice daily in the magical show at Christmas. After four weeks the Magician, the Great Masoni called me into his dressing room to see him. He said, 'We can't afford to take you on tour, but I've got you another job' and I said, 'Oh, that's great is it, what show is it?' He said, 'It's not exactly a show'. I said, 'Oh is it sort of back stage?' He said, 'Well, not exactly'. I said, 'Is it sort of Front of House?' He said, 'Not exactly' He said, 'An assistant night watchman in a factory in Croydon!' I said, 'Oh.' I sounded a bit disappointed. He said, 'On the other hand you could come with us on tour if you're willing to be Assistant Stage Manager, Property Master, do the Get In and the Get Out, work the follow spot, look after the animals and take a cut in Salary?' I was 16 years of age and wanted to be in Show Business, so of course I agreed.

Did you get any training at all when you were in the theatre?

No, I never had an Acting, Singing or Dancing lesson in my life. I went on with this tour working twenty-four hours a day making myself indispensable, doing everything for this magician. That was in the theatre from morning until night. And then there was an advertisement in The Stage newspaper which said, 'Boy Wanted, must be over 15 years of age, under 5-foot-tall, must be able to sing and dance for a West End musical going on tour'. Apart from the singing and the dancing, I was perfect.

This lovely old lady, Miss Terry said to me, "Can you sing?" I said "No Miss Terry". She said "Can you dance?" I said "No Miss Terry". And she said "You've got the job!" The show was "Dear Miss Phoebe" and I became one of the famous "Terry's Juveniles". Eventually after a three-month Number One theatre tour of the UK, the show folded. Then Miss Terry got me a job as Bonzo the Dog in Pantomime. But I realised I needed to learn the business, so I asked company manager, actor Stuart Saunders, if he could put me in touch with an agent – which he did – a famous agent at that time for young people. I was 16 years of age, but looked younger. She got me special guest weeks with repertory companies across the UK. I was very lucky as most people that work in rep stay with them for 6 months, a year, two or three or more. I was able to work with a different company and different directors by just doing one production and then moving on to somewhere else.

It was a great proving ground for me, working in those companies for a salary of £10 a week. Many of the actors that I worked with at the time went on to become big stars – actors such as Frank Findlay and Edward Woodward.

So how did you break through onto TV?

I got in as a lie because there was yet another advertisement in yet another newspaper that said 'Boy wanted for television series - must be Welsh, only actors with Welsh accents need apply' so I went to see this director - a woman called Naomi Capon, and I put on a Welsh accent and got the job. On the first day of rehearsals I said to her 'I'm not Welsh I'm Cockney' and she said, 'Well, you convinced me so let's see if you can convince the audience' and she let me carry on and that was my first job in television on a lie.

You broke into films – the first being "The Curse of Frankenstein"?

Yeah, I played Peter Cushing as a young man in 'The Curse of Frankenstein' so I am the youngest Frankenstein in the world. Then

I got to work with a famous Director called J. Lee Thompson. He did 'Guns of Navaronne', 'Ice Cold in Alex' and several more wonderful films. I did, I think, one line in a picture called 'The Good Companions' and then the next picture I did for him was 'Woman in a Dressing Gown', my part was over as the Director's credit hit the screen. My third film that I made with him was called "No Trees in the Street" – I had a starring role in that one… and a seven-year film contract with Associated British and I went on to do "The Young Ones", "Summer Holiday", "Wonderful Life", and "Crooks in Cloisters" under that contract.

Did you have to screen test for the Cliff Richard films?

No, it's very funny actually. I got this call to go to meet the Director and Producer of the picture which had the working title "The Cliff Richard Story" which obviously became 'The Young Ones' eventually. The last time I'd seen the director was when I'd interviewed him on a television show, "The Sunday Break" – about a short film that he'd made in Canada. He was

worried at that time whether he was going to reclaim his train fare to the TV Studios. When I met him to talk about the Cliff Richard film, He asked me what I'd being doing work wise… I asked him if he ever got his expenses. He couldn't wait for me to leave the office! That Director was Syd Furie.

'The Young Ones' was a number two box office hit in Great Britain that year. Number one was "Guns of Navarone".

So, I continued to do theatre, television, film, radio and I suppose the busiest period was from the 60s, 70s and 80s and then of course I got involved because of doing 'It Ain't Half Hot Mum'.

How did you get the part of Gloria in "It Ain't Half Hot Mum"?

Well, I was unemployed and so I got a job teaching at the drama school "Italia Conte". One of my pupils was a thirteen-year-old Lesley Ash. I didn't know what I was doing- sort of hanging on by the seat of my pants and one day one of the teachers said to me "My Husband is doing a pilot for a new TV series, you'd be marvellous in it!" And I said, "What's it called?" she said, "At the moment the working title is 'It Ain't Half Hot Mum'. She said, "There's a part a character called Gloria and you'd be wonderful!"

So, I went along to see David Croft and Jimmy Perry and Jim asked me so many questions about all sorts of things and David, whom I had worked for before, just had one question. All he said to me was could you just lift your hair off your forehead please. So a couple of years after we'd been in the show they did this is your

life on David Croft and what had happened he said the reason why I had asked you to do that was because I wanted to see if you combed your hair forward, whether you were bald because if it was a success I didn't want sort of old men coming in and then being too old for it all. I told him it was still growing very healthily – and it still is!

What was it like working on 'It Ain't Half Hot Mum' was it quite a fun show to do?

Oh yes, it was great because you're in the hands of David Croft who was a genius. He'd come to rehearsals and he'd sit and laugh and each day even when he's heard the joke a dozen times, so you still thought you were being funny. Jimmy Perry the co-writer with David also came to every rehearsal. There was a programme on the other night about the pair of them and it was so accurate. I didn't realise that when they tested a reaction towards a pilot of 'Dad's Army,' it wasn't the glowing report that they'd expected so David hid it until such times that it was too late from stopping the first episode from going to air and being the enormous success, it eventually became.

I always thought that it should've got an award just for the set because it always looked so hot - before every take they would spray a solution of water and glycerine on to us. On our backs, our chests and on our faces. They said that's all we've got going for us because if we'd been out there in the jungle during the war, we'd have been soaking wet within thirty-seconds.

The saddest thing about the show is that it will never be repeated in this country. At the moment it's showing in New Zealand, Australia, Dubai, Hong Kong, Holland and yet not in this country for a couple of reasons. One because the sergeant called us "poofs" and the other is because a white man played a black man. Michael Bates, a great actor who played one of the Indian aids – but he was born in India, spoke Urdu fluently. There was an Indian actor who said at the time that you should have got an Indian actor to play him until he saw Michael's performance. Then he said, "not none of us could have portrayed the character so well!". David and Jimmy, right up to the time of their deaths were trying to get it repeated. They said another generation should have had a chance to see it. The pair of them always said that out of all of their shows, "It Ain't Half Hot Mum!" was their favourite – they had both been in the army and had been involved with concert parties.

You've done a lot of voice acting for children's shows – such as Super Ted? What was it like to do that compared to acting?

It's still acting but just in another form. I did "Skeleton's' voice in "Super Ted". I got that job after doing a fifteen-week pantomime season at the famous London Palladium. Windsor Davies and I were playing "Captain and Mate in "Dick Whittington". Playing the villain was the lovely actor Victor Spinetti. His cousin was Mike Young who created "Super Ted" and he asked me if I could

do the voice for Skeleton. I just took "Gloria" to another level as a starter and found the character from there. Even though it's just your voice that can be heard, you tend to do the actions to achieve the end result. But obviously you don't have to worry about walking into furniture and that sort of thing!

Do you still keep in touch with people like Windsor Davies at all?

Do you know I haven't? One works with so many people over the years that while you work with them, they are like your family. But when a production finishes, you go into the next one. And a new family… I occasionally bump into Cliff Richard at charity events. The last time I met him was at Buckingham Palace!

What are you working on at the moment?

I'm still writing my book which I started almost 35 years ago. Show-business has changed so much since I started. I once said "when I started in Television, it was "Joe Public" sitting at home watching professionals, and now it's out of work professionals sitting at home watching "Joe Public" – Too many reality shows. When I started as a kid of 15 all I wanted to do is act. I just enjoy acting. But today people just want to be famous.

About a year ago I was working on a Cruise Ship. I had to do an hour spot on stage. While on board I met a lovely couple and we spent some time together. I asked them what they did work wise. They said "We're on a TV show, "The only way is Essex". I said "That's nice, it must be fun?" And they said "We're Extras and we sit in the background. So, we don't have speaking parts." I said "When do you know when you are working?" They said "The phone will ring and the production company will say, "Can you be in such and such a place tomorrow morning?" – They didn't get paid. They didn't get any expenses. If they were lucky, they got a cup of tea!

That's a true story – that's Joe Public spending their own money to be on Television – in the background! But they were happy.

I'm just glad I'm not starting in this Profession and that I've enjoyed being employed in all of my working life!

40

GODLEY & CREME

first got interested in the music of Godley and Crème after seeing
e video of "Cry" – music videos had been around for a while of
urse, but they were usually bland affairs. The video for Cry had
veryone in the room transfixed, and I decided I would investigate
e band further. The duo that formed Godley and Crème (Kevin
odley and Lol Crème) were previously part of the amazing 10cc
ith hits such as "I'm not in love" and "I'm Mandy – Fly me".

Kevin
Godley

Kevin Godley has had many hits over the years, as well as
ecoming a successful music video director and editor.

Shaun: Both 10cc and Godley and Crème didn't seem to propagate any particular image – was this intentional?

We never even thought about it. I think it was probably because we weren't in the thick of it. We were working outside of London which was, is and probably always will be the centre of the music business in the UK. We were stuck out in the outskirts of Manchester and there wasn't much of a scene going on there particularly and we were four guys who were interested in making interesting music; the thought of constructing an image for us never really entered the picture. We were obviously aware of what was going on elsewhere with people like Gary Glitter, Sweet and all the other maniacs that were out there but it never really appealed to us because we were too focused on audio.

Hilary: You all played instruments and you were all proficient song writers - did that cause any conflict because all of you could do everything?

No, strangely enough it didn't because I suppose we all had our basic roles which were the basic instruments that we played but I could only ever play drums and sing. The others could maybe play bass, keyboards and guitar so that was never anything that impacted on me so I never had that problem.

What we did was always decided by who could do it the best and it was a very democratic way of working. So for instance if there was a song that was written on piano then the person that played it on piano in the first place got to play it to begin with, because he was more familiar with it; however if one of the members of the band that could play the piano could contribute a better version of it, then he would be the one that would play the piano.

The trickiest bits were the vocals because all four of us were singers so what tended to happen was each of us would audition for the role of lead singer for the song. One of us would go into the studio and attempt to sing it and if it wasn't so good the rest would hold up a sign saying 'Next'. So that was kind of how we approached everything we did.

Hilary: What was your favourite 10cc song?

Gosh! Well, it's a very difficult question to answer because there are lots of favourites for different reasons. I suppose the obvious answer would be 'I'm not in love' because it turned out so much better than we expected it to. The original version, the first recorded version, was pretty crappy. We all agreed it was pretty crappy so it was shelved. It was only when we came back to it when I suggested doing it with all voices that it took on a life of its own and the production produced itself after a while - that was our most successful song.

There are other songs such as 'Somewhere in Hollywood' – they are favourites for different reasons because as songwriters they challenge the song writing process and I felt that we pushed ourselves to the limit on those two particular tracks.

Shaun: So how did you get that sound on 'I'm not in love'?

Once we'd agreed that we were going to go for an all encompassing vocal sound then we had to figure out how to do it - there were only four of us. So rather than hire a choir, which was the obvious option, we decided we'd do it ourselves! Myself, Lol and Graham went into the studio, stood around a mic and sung a note that was needed for the song, just one note for as long as we could sing it. We did that note 16 times on the 16 track tape recorder, mixed it down to two tracks on the quarter inch tape recorder and created a tape loop out of it. We did that for every note that we'd need for the song; it took about 3 weeks to do. We recorded each of the loops back onto the 16 track so effectively that the 16 track machine became a voice sample instrument and we used the faders on the control board to create chords on the notes that we'd sung. We'd fade them in and out through the backing tracks which we'd done with an electric piano, electric guitar and a moog synthesizer bass drum. We just faded them in and out to that rough backing track and that's what created the sound.

We were one of the first bands to get hold of a Moog synthesiser when they came in to the UK, but we didn't use it that much and we didn't use its full capabilities. We used it , like a lot of people did , to create odd effects here and there. I think the reason we used it on 'I'm not in Love' was because it meant I could play a bass drum in the control room because that's where the electric piano and the guitar were being played so we could all be together in the one space rather than be out in the live area and on full kit. We probably mostly used it to add effect or to simulate sounds that we couldn't get using ordinary instruments.

Shaun: One minute you're in a band and the next minute you're bringing out these brilliant videos! I think the first

one I saw was 'Cry'. Did you have any interest in doing any video before the music?

No, because the medium didn't really exist. Before we were in the band, Lol Creme and I were at Art college together studying graphic design so we have a sort of visual background and we had left that behind once the band became successful.

I think a lot of the music that we wrote was very cinematic, very filmic, and it was our way of making films with sound. We didn't have access to the real things to make films with back then so we did sound things instead. But once we were on our own (as Godley and Crème, after leaving 10cc), we started recording our own music. We weren't a touring band; we were just two guys recording - so we couldn't go out and promote them as a band as such.

We figured it might be interesting to make little films to promote them -although there weren't that many places where they could be seen back – this was before MTV and other such channels. We had an idea for a film for one of our early singles called 'An Englishman in New York' and we went to the record company with the idea fully expecting them to say "piss off" but they said "Yes, why not? But you can't direct it on your own because you've never done it before so you have to get a proper director in to do it". They got one in for us and we made the film and we learnt a lot about cameras editing, lighting, everything really during the process. At the end of that whole thing we looked at each

other and thought, '"Hang on a minute... whatever this is, we can do some interesting things with this stuff called video". Not many people were doing it and record labels didn't know if there was any value in doing them. Before then they had only been used because a band wasn't available to appear live on some show or other so various people made interesting little films instead as a substitute.

That's how it all started but for us it was the first time we'd been in at the beginning of the movement because when we got into music it was already well into its stride, but here was something interesting and new happening. I think we helped helped to form it in some way.

Shaun: Do you think your lack of any formal training in film-making helped in a way because it meant that you didn't think of anything as a barrier so you just sort of tried things out?

Yeah, we shared that approach with Orson Welles, strangely enough. What he did was quite revolutionary at the time - he did it because he didn't know he couldn't! No one told him he couldn't and, because he didn't know the rules, he just made it up as he went along. He made things that he thought would look good and that's pretty much what we did. We bent the technology to our needs.

Hilary: You've made videos with many diverse people from Marti Pellow and Wet Wet Wet through to Snow Patrol and some reality show winners like Will Young, which is one of my favourite videos of all

time. I believe you also made the 'Frankie Goes to Hollywood' Two Tribes video. How was it and what was the creative process? Did you have the majority of the say or did the artists have input as well?

It's a selfish process. Obviously it involves listening to the music a lot and just kind of freewheeling with it. I wanted to see if I could come up with something that was something that I would like to see and I felt that it would be appropiate for the music and also would be something that the artist could carry off then I would assume that it's worth pitching that idea. Often I didn't but sometimes I did. It had to fulfill those criteria, the first being – "Is it something that I would like to see?" Because if it doesn't exist yet, is this idea fermenting something that would be interesting? That's pretty much the process once you've actually thought of the idea; there's then a number of things that you have to do and it's the same now as it was then even though there is so much more "noise" now. You think of the idea and then you talk to your producer, who has to then go and tell you whether the budget is sufficient to make your idea work. Then chat with the video commissioner, who is the person from either the label or the managment company who had commissioned me to come up with the idea, to see if they felt that this might be something that the band might like. You pitch it and then you wait and wait and wait.Then 9 times out of 10 they come back and say we've actually changed the track, we're gonna release this one instead or they say, "Let's do it!" There are so many moving parts to the process.

To go back to your initial question, it's just a matter of sitting there and thinking or allowing the music to touch you in some way and I suppose if you've been doing what I've been doing for a while it's kind of an automatic process. If you have a feel for it you know something will come eventually and that's how it works.

Shaun: *Video editing software is amazing – but do you think having that level of power to manipulate film now (often quite easily) can make the process worse?*

I wouldn't say it's worse. What I would say is that I would prefer to live in what I would call a digi-logue world where there could be a combination of the best of digital and the best of analogue because editing video to me is very much like playing an instrument and it always has been. It's been a very musical experience and initially editing suites were very analogue places. If you wanted to cut between two shots you pressed a button, and if you wanted to mix between two shots you operated this little paddle - you could modulate how you actually did that by hand and that's all disappeared. That's now been taken away and replaced with a guy sat next to you punching in numbers which isn't quite as satisfying and it takes longer. Everything takes longer now because you can defer making a decision. You have a good shot and you think "Well, let's shave a bit off both ends of the shot and maybe let's try the shot here instead of there, let's flip it left to right, turn it upside down". In other words your choices are infinite so you're using the ability to try it in lots of different ways so inevitably something that used to take us 24 hours to edit now takes 3 days. The job expands to fill the time allotted to it. You've got 3 days to edit so I'll take 3 days.

I think the other major difference between now and the earlier days is that there never used to be a critique process from the client. A director was hired because they'd made some good films and whoever was hiring you recognised that you had a particular way of looking at the world that may be appropriate for the song. So you were given the song and you went away and did it and handed it in and that was it there was no "Well, we need a little bit more of the singer and you know the drummer looks a bit pale so can you maybe give him a bit more colour". There was none of that kind of involvment from the commercial powers that be. That is so much more dominant today than it was with the marketing departments. Everybody thinks they know what works.

Shaun: *They are trying to do an artistic decision by comittee basically?*

Yeah in a word. That happens across the board. It happens at the beginning, the middle and the end which is why I don't do many of them any more because it's harder to be as creative as one used to be because everyone's so cautious. It's crazy. It doesn't make any sense to me why everyone's cautious.

"We want to be really edgy and do something really dark," but what they really mean is, they want something that's as close to the last thing that their artist did that was a success. We've reached saturation point.

Hilary: *Are a lot of the artists very protective of their image?*

44

cool. It has to be kind of within the scope of what people anticipate from you.

Hilary: 'Whole World Band' -What was all that about?

That came from a music special for BBC back in 1989. They were running a two or three week special about environmental concerns and they were looking for an idea to show communities and countries working together but at a musical level. The series was called 'One World Fortnight' and they wanted to do a kind of 'Live Aid' concert thing with people from all over the world appearing but that had kind of been done so my idea was to film what I called a 'chain tape'. The idea was to begin a piece of music in one place and film it taking place, then take that footage and the sound around the world adding artists as we travelled. I never for one second remotely expected them to green light it but they did. so there was a programme that went out called 'One World, One Voice' in 1989 on BBC2. Around 2008, I'm thinking about the potential of the internet and what it could and couldn't do, and I figured, "What if one could actually do that without travelling? What if you could put a piece of music up, a little filmed clip of somebody playing the guitar and singing, and then what if someone in Guatemala could add an overdub to it in sound and picture, and then someone

I think it depends who the artist is and I think a lot of artists are totally in control of what they do and they are the people that you deal with. Some other artists are controlled by management and record labels and they've become "hit machines." You know you have to do something cool but not that

in Scotland could add drums to it in sound and picture?" That's the genesis of the idea and that's how it works and so 'Whole World Band' came from 'One World, One Voice' in 1989.

Hilary: And is the 'Muscle Memory' a continuation of that idea really?

Well I suppose I enjoy the idea of collaboration because the only instrument that I play is drums; it's not the ideal instrument to write songs with. I am always looking for interesting ways to collaborate but the idea for 'Muscle Memory' came from a couple of people, whom I'd never met, sending me a couple of pieces of instrumental music and asking if I'd be interested in turning them into songs. I had never worked that way before. Essentially it was remote collaboration so I tried it and I really enjoyed the process and it worked really well. So having a desire to make an album, I thought that that might be an interesting way to go about it. I'd ask people to send me instrumental tracks that I would then convert in to songs and then I would perform the songs, little realising that I would get about 284 of them which was crazy! But it's been great! It's been amazing. Normally it's sitting opposite somebody who would play piano, or they'd play a guitar and you'd react and bounce an idea backwards and forwards till it worked. Then you'd move on to another bit then you'd maybe scrap it and start again. It was real time one on one situation. But this, this was different. This was essentially being handed a drawing in black and white and saying 'Fill in all the colours. But the drawing exists, you know? This is what you are working with pal, you can't deviate from it!' And that's a fascinating way to work! I've not met any of these people before and I took great care when the music came in not to investigate who they were. I only wanted to see that the music that they had sent inspired me in some way. It was only once I begun to pick songs that I knew were going to work that I then made contact with them and we would talk and begin the process at a slightly deeper level.

Shaun: *So how many of the 280 odd did you end up making into songs?*

I mean to do an album so it's probably gonna be 12 or 14 and I'm 11 in so far. I'm waiting for a couple of people to get back to me with some questions I have. It's taken some time because when I began the process I had never done anything like that before. I'd never written a melody and lyrics on my own before. I had always worked in conjunction with someone from the very beginning of the process and this way I am coming in half way through the process. It's a conversion thing that I am doing. I am turning something that exists as this into something that exists as that, so there was a lot of confidence building to be done on my part to get used to the new way of doing it and believe that I could do it. I wouldn't say that I found it easy but I found it stunningly exciting to do. I'm still right in the middle of it and it's great; it's given me a new lease of musical life.

The other interesting thing is there is no one to tell me what to do. There is no one to say "That sounds like shit so why don't you try it this way." or "You can't say that, try saying this," There's none of that so I'm just doing it by instinct, which is always much better than thinking when writing music. I think it's going to be good.

I'm not trying to make it sound anything in particular or specific. I am being driven by each piece that I am given. But I think it sounds reasonably valid. I think

it sounds like music that should exist now as opposed to music that existed forty years ago which is always a problem with artists of my age. I guess a lot of people that come from my era tend to stick in that era musically but I've taken on board everything that's happened since and I am open to anything so I try and bring that to what I am doing now.

Shaun: *Once the album is finished, will you perform it on stage? And how would that work bearing in mind the many collaborators?*

If I did, it certainly wouldn't be in a traditional way. It doesn't have to be performed by everyone who wrote the tracks, but I don't think I would be into putting a band together and going on the road in that respect. I might figure out another way of doing it which might be more interesting and more practical for me but, you know, it's a little early to talk about that. I've got to get to the end of stage one first.

Shaun: *Do you think the current culture of downloading music has killed the art of album making?*

Yeah, I think we are losing a lot of things with the age of the instant download. This generation we are spoilt essentially. One doesn't want to dwell on the past but I remember when I was a kid and the artist that I loved would release records, then you would queue up all night to get them when they hit the shop! You would take them home and play them to death. You would analyse and soak up every note and every word, and there would be a sort of spiritual and physical attachment to this piece of music.

That doesn't really happen too much any more because there's so much of it and, as you quite rightly say, it is so available. It's the same with anything if you get too much of anything. If you eat too much food, you get fat and ill. If you get too much money, you get lazy. It's across the board and now you've got too much music. The recording industry is suffering too, because it's not valuable anymore. People don't get remunerated in the same level that they did. Music should be on a par with a great painting or a great sculpture. We've lost the sense of rarity. The sense of anticipation has gone.

Shaun: *So many of the modern records are generic sounding, to my ears – What do you think?*

They are. It's like there are some people somewhere who have analysed what makes a hit record, how many beats per minute work and what sort of drum patterns work. I guess you're right as you do tend to get a lot of this kind of record. It's not exactly the same but it's got similar elements because they know it works. It's very rare that you find a track or an artist that really stands out.

I think audiences are a little scared of something that is unlike everything else. They've been merged into consumers - people consume music as if it was a burger - it's just the way things are but when we started making music, the music then was a pre-eminent force for youth culture. It's not now. Music is just one of many forms of entertainment alongside TV, the video games, VR, AR and so on and so forth. It's just part of the spectrum that's enlarged beyond anything we could have known back then. Music is just a fraction of a way of diverting something in the world.

SPACE: 1999

Space: 1999 was a Science Fiction series from the workshops of Gerry Anderson (who also made many "Super Marionette" based shows, such as Fireball XL5 and The Thunderbirds. Space 1999 though, like UFO, featured human actors, and starred real-life husband and wife team of Martin Landau and Barbera Bain as Commander Koenig, and Dr Helena Russell respectively. They led the crew of Moonbase Alpha through many hostile alien encounters and natural disasters.

What was not to like about it? It had Spaceships! It had laser beams! It had more Spaceships! But unlike a lot of the Science Fiction that I'd seen before it, there were often spiritual elements, and moral dilemmas that went beyond the corny Star Trek themes.

Martin Bower

Martin Bower was one of the men behind the models made for the show – responsible mostly for the alien vessels. He also made models and props for many other programmes such as Blakes 7, The Tomorrow People, and films such as Alien, and Outland.

Were you quite creative as a child?

Yes, I was. My grandpa was chief electrician at the Whitehall Theatre in London for 42 years and they did a show called "DRY ROT". In this play they had to break down a door in every performance. This meant I got loads of blocks and sheets of balsa wood, so I started to carve them into shapes. That was in 1960 when I was already making flying models from other materials – mostly the traditional boats and planes.

I was also watching a lot of science fiction on television, and I began experimenting with special effects - I used to put a certain mixture of 2 easily available "household granules"(I'm not allowed by law to say what they were now). But when mixed together would either explode or, if put into a metal tube, would shoot out a jet of flame and smoke! So, I was a "Pyromaniac" at 8 years old! I very nearly blew our shed up when one experiment didn't quite go to plan!

Did anyone give you any training?

No. All self-taught. I think I got it from my mother's side as my dad couldn't cut a straight line! I started on the Airfix kits, but soon began making my own models. I was a big fan of Supercar, the Gerry Anderson series, and this inspired me to have a go at making my own Supercar, plus other models too. My Dad let me commandeer the shed, and even eventually bought me a lathe (which I still own and use by the way!).

To begin with my Dad was a bit worried about me using power tools – I was just a young lad – and said "let me do the work, if you tell me what to do" but it

wasn't the same, so in the end he trusted me to not take my own fingers off and let me get on with it. I got a lot more experienced, and I did go and work for a set design company for few weeks, but instead of learning about sets and so on, I found myself nailing canvases to wooden frames all day.

I did eventually find a job creating scale models of traditional craft such as Boeing 747's, ships and helicopters – the company would sell these for display in travel agency windows. I did actually apply for a job at the BBC in their special effects department – I simply turned up with photos of my models, but I was told that due to safety regulations (and more than likely union regulations) I was too young (I was 17) – which was annoying. I had to be 21 to work for that department. But I did have a chance meeting with the producer of "Blue Peter" – Biddy Baxter – in the elevator on the way out. And long story short, I was in one of the episodes, showing off a model of the Apollo 11 Rocket that I'd made.

So how did you get your break into Space: 1999?

I got onto "SPACE: 1999" (my first Science Fiction work) by seeing a story in the newspaper that said "THUNDERBIRDS MAN TO FILM NEW TV SERIES" – Obviously I was very much "into" Gerry Anderson's work, so I found the address and I wrote to them. I was told to go and see Brian Johnson, (the Special Effects Supervisor).

I went down to Bray Studios, with one large model I'd built (a long battlecruiser that looked a bit like the ship in 2001: A Space Odyssey), and a load of photos. Brian looked at my photos and then asked me to get the large spacecraft model I'd bought down with me, and said he wanted to shoot some test-footage of the

model I'd actually made at age 16! So, I was quite amazed at this.

The test footage looked excellent. He then told me he wanted to buy the model off of me (which ended up appearing in 5 episodes of Space: 1999 – with various modifications for each episode), and he offered me the job of building models needed for each week's episode.

The first script he gave me was for "Alpha Child", which was the seventh episode of Season 1, and I asked "When do you want them by?" and Brian said "Two weeks' time". I thought nothing of this at the time because I was so excited. I had a quick look at the script, and saw that there were two ships involved, including the battlecruiser that I'd just handed over.

In this episode, the "Alphans" (The moonbase crew) celebrate the arrival of the first child to be born in the base. But of course, things turn strange – the kid grows up rather quickly, and then some alien ships arrive – he was an alien imposter all along.

I was driving home, head in the clouds about the new job, but as time progressed it began to dawn on me more and more exactly how much work I had to do and how little time I had to do it!

By this time, my family (that I still lived with) were living in a home with an old Tractor barn, and my parents had given me one area of it to use as my workshop. I did all of the models for Space: 1999 from there. It was a bit like a potting shed, but was wood-lined and very nice. Well, I had a design in mind for the alien ship that I'd already been working on, sort of based on a Manta Ray shape, but

with a cut out in the front and an enormous gun that sticks out, that lit up from the inside.

I posted Brian the drawing, and called him a day later to check he had received it, and he had and said the design was fine, so with the tight schedule already in-place I got to work. I'd been told about how to place the mounts for the ship (to aid movement and to stop it falling to bits), and I got to work.

Once I'd completed it, I took it down to show Brian, who loved it. But asked me to build another one half the size (this was standard practice, later found out. This was for distance shots, and moving the camera further away from the bigger model can create a lot of focusing problems and also there wasn't a great deal of room in the studio).

I had a heart attack. I raced home, and got to work – I worked through the night and completed it a couple of days later.

Space: 1999 looked amazing. I loved the modular design. What sort of brief or outline were you given?

Almost all of the moonbase models were made by Brian Johnson – we wanted all of the Earth ships to look like they came

out of the same factory to give them a certain "standardised" look – that was where the modular design elements (particularly the nose of the eagles) came from.

As I said, Brian Johnson (and Nicky Allder to a lesser extent) were responsible for the vast majority of those. Well, I was given the script of course, and the parts that were important to the ship design were underlined or highlighted by Brian. My role was to do the alien craft that crossed the path of the crew – so – because they were aliens, I could use a lot more of my imagination to create the craft – though sometimes Brian Johnson would give me a drawing if he had something specific in mind... But by series 2 he more or less knew I'd come up with a good-looking model based on a script in time for filming. I would always create a few drawings before starting the work. One thing that Brian appreciated from me was that I would spend time weathering the craft. This makes them look like a real craft that has been used. If you get the pencil lead and rub it onto a tissue and then smudge areas of the craft or vehicle, it dirties it up a bit and makes it look like it's been subjected to weather conditions and had a bit of wear and tear. Brian had to do the weathering himself with other model makers, so I always saved him a bit of time by doing it myself!

He would give me the next script each time I delivered the latest model. So, I was building them very fast. I only realised afterwards that I hadn't taken many photos of the building process as there just wasn't time.

What sort of things do you need to take into consideration when building the craft, especially for TV?

Firstly, it has to be strong; for instance, all girder-work had to be done in brass tube soldered together. Then it needs mounting points. These are places where a rig can be plugged into the model so it can be suspended while being filmed, with no need for wires. I only built three model "Space Eagles" One was a plastic breakaway model that broke apart when it was crashed. Then there was a 5-inch model for one episode that had to be swallowed by a huge shuttle-like craft, and then a 22-inch brass and Perspex model simply because we only had one and it was better to have an extra one.

How heavy are the Space: 1999 models? What are they made of?

Well a 44-inch Eagle weighed around 30-40 pounds when loaded with cannisters of freon gas, but taking say the "SUPERSWIFT", essentially, I would carve the nose (Command module) in jelutong wood. And it would stay as wood as there was not enough time to take moulds as the 5ft model has to be built in only about 3 weeks. This is a wood that is excellent for getting a good paint finish on and it's strong.

Then the main body was built onto a frame. I used a great deal of what is known as EMA Model Supplies plastic tube to build

fuel and oxygen tanks and some carefully chosen fine kit parts. There are far too many people out there that use loads of plastic kits that can easily be recognised on screen.

I would also look out for interestingly shaped objects that were part of light fittings or even food or cleaning packaging which I could cannibalise to make areas of detail on the larger wooden and brass models – engine parts, radar dishes, or even just grills and hatches. After a while you get really good at spotting things like that, and my workshop still has boxes of odds and ends that I refuse to throw away – they will all end up as part of a space ship or something one day.

Even some of the ships we made would be reused – there is a "ships graveyard" in the episode "Dragon's Domain" that uses alien ships from other episodes – repainted though to make them look a little bit different. The speed we shot the series meant that this was the only way we could do it.

But we were quite ambitious in many respects too – we would film parts of ships undocking using claws that would open up to release pods (actually that was used in "Dragon's Domain" too) – so it was about time management – very important with the time scales we had to work in. We had around two weeks to do each show.

What would you say the difference is between making a display model and a model used in filming?

No difference at all in my case. Size perhaps, depending on the

scale needed if it is a display model – film models are usually created in at least two sizes, but sometimes three – the largest one is usually around twelve-foot-long. And of course, display models don't need mounting points because you're not going to be lifting them and moving them around, so things won't usually break off.

I build the film models just as detailed as the static display models though – more so really if the scale is massive. Even if a model's fine details aren't obvious on the screen, I know the Director is still going to be looking at it really close up to check for quality, and it has to be well-detailed for that reason alone.

Which other model makers do you really admire?

Steve Howarth in the UK – He's done some amazing work over the years – He's got a good design sense. He has worked on TV shows such as Space Precinct, Dr Who, Red Dwarf, but also film work – Aliens Vs. Predator, The film version of Hitchhikers Guide to the Galaxy. Technically very good, and is very clever in the way that he applies detail – the golden rule is to "not stick bits of detail on unless there is a REASON for it to be there" and Steve manages to put in just about the correct level of detail into his models, and makes them look like functional units. You don't have to spell everything out, and Steve is very good at that. But Steve is unlike me in that he'll spend time drawing really accurate technical drawings before he begins the job of modelling. Maybe he has the advantage of time though? I never had that luxury.

Greg Jein in the USA is another person I admire intensely – he has

worked on some classics, such as Close Encounters of the Third Kind, V, Hunt for Red October, Firefox, Batteries not included, and several Star Trek films and series models too. Again, the detail and practicality are what I admire about his work – He has a much looser style to his work than Steve. He doesn't use machinery to make his models, which I find incredible. He also has a great sense of humour. The scene with the absolutely colossal alien ship at the end of Close Encounters was filled with detail – and Greg had bought hundreds of commercial model kits to help him fill the details in – if you look really closely you can see little R2D2's from Star Wars – too small to see in the film, but if you take a look at the model itself, you can clearly see them. Also, the centre of the ship, which is about 4 or 5 feet in diameter – there are probes sticking out from it. And again, you can't recognise them in the film, but if you see the model, there are two toothbrushes that form some of these amazing looking antennae.

Are there any TV shows or films that you wished you had worked on?

Yep, rather obviously "2001: A Space Odyssey". But if I'd been born earlier, I'd have liked to have done "The War of the Worlds" as the film starring Gene Barry is not very good and the model work is (in my opinion) very poor. Some 30 years ago I was involved in a photo novel of "The War of the Worlds" where I'd built and designed the Martian Fighting Machines and lesser known "Handling Machines". I built them all to scales and shot about 50 photos taken from scenes in the book. But then Jeff Wayne bought the rights to do his music album and the project was shelved.

You worked on Alien, among other projects. Which designs were you responsible for?

Well, I designed the front of the "Narcissus" (the escape pod shown at the very end of the film), but only the front. The reason for this was that the set of the back of "Narcissus" had already been filmed, as they'd built a foreshortened mock-up of the back for the scenes where Ripley shoots the Alien out into space. It's not noticeable in the film, but that set was only half the length it was supposed to be, but it looked fine from the back. I built the Narcissus as part of a team. I also did a lot of the detail work on the refinery (again, with a few other modellers).

We had a crew that changed around as the film evolved. Also, only 5 months into shooting, Brian Johnson was called to the States to be Special Effects Supervisor on "The Empire Strikes Back". So, Nicky Allder took over. After Brian left the models, I think I'd use the word "evolved" because that's exactly what happened. We built and filmed the Nostromo in yellow paintwork for five months, then once Ridley Scott had finished principal photography on Alien at Shepperton Studios, he came over to Bray Studios (where we were working). And he made a few changes to the story and to some of the models.

The first thing he did was to paint the Nostromo grey and then weather it down so it was quite dark.

So, we had to change the models a lot. This also included the Nostromo's undocking arm. In discussions with Ridley, he said he'd like to have an enormous claw like arm that extended and then opened and released the Nostromo from the Refinery.

I had to create the model, starting with a working mechanical grabbing arm that Nicky Allder created – I used that as a base, and added detail to it.

What are you working on these days?

I've just done 3 large spacecraft for Red Dwarf. I also have several private commissions too. I keep busy, and there is a large fan base of people that like to have models from the shows and films I have worked on – I was fortunate in that I always kept plans and lots of photos of everything I made. We're also working on a book about my work too!

PIERS ANTHONY
A SPELL FOR CHAMELEON

The First Xanth Novel

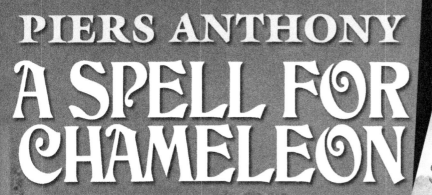

My friend Ian, who was a little older than myself, would introduce me to reading as a genuine leisure pursuit when I was around 10 years old. We both joined the local library. There was an entire shelf of the "Xanth" series of fantasy books – I was first of all attracted to the fantastic cover-art of course, but having read a few, the characters grew on me, and I was soon lost in their magical world.

Piers Anthony

Piers Anthony is the author of the ever expanding Xanth series, amongst other books, and was kind enough to let us interview him....

You were separated from your parents for a while whilst they were in Spain during the Civil war. Did this impact upon your early childhood?

Yes and no. My first memory is of the nanny who took care of my sister and I. Separation from her was perhaps the greatest grief of my early life; I never really got over it. It was as if I had been adopted into a new family. Sometimes I wished that it would all turn out to be a bad dream and I'd wake up and find myself back in England with her. I understand that serious writers usually have suffered an extended privation in childhood; it is as if they are compelled to write to make up for what can never be set entirely right. It is called the gift that keeps giving, ironically. It is true for me too.

What originally sparked your interest to become an author? Did you have any favourite authors?

I find this hard to believe myself, but as a child I did not dream of being a writer. It was not until I was two years into college. I had to choose a major for my final two years for my BA degree and I realised that since my other options, like Art, Psychology, or Higher Maths, had been closed out by circumstances I did not control, writing was what was left. I pondered a day and a night. It was far from being a desolate decision; it was like a light turning on, illuminating my ambition, and it has guided me ever since. The promise had always been there; I simply had not realised it. Now I shudder to think how readily I could have failed to discover that profession. I did admire science fiction and fantasy writers like Theodore Sturgeon, Robert Heinlein, Jack Williamson and many others, but they were not my inspiration to join them. It was more like a goat discovering by accident that there was a way to escape the corral and taking the road less travelled. I have had one of the rougher courses as an author, such as getting blacklisted for six years because I protested about getting cheated by a publisher, and I remain militant about publishing malfeasance, but I never regretted becoming a writer.

You lived on a simple "back to the land" community as a child – Did you enjoy the experience?

No. It was not that it was bad. I did not enjoy my childhood overall, as evidenced by the fact that I wet my bed for years and suffered compulsive twitches of my head and hands. These were not physical disorders, but emotional ones. I privately assessed my life up to about age twelve and concluded that if I had a choice to relive it exactly as it had been, or never to exist at all, I would prefer the latter. Apart from that, life on the farm was good, and I retain a liking for the forest. The farm had goats, and I think goats are fine animals. Today I live on a small tree farm I own, and my sister and I are researching and writing a history of that failed utopian effort.

What did you take from the author Scott Nearing that you met there? Did he have any influence over your future writing style? He sounds like an interesting character.

I think it was on my eighth birthday when I went to Scott Nearing's farm to buy some maple sugar, as he was in that business among others. I mentioned that it was my birthday, and he said, "Mine too." So it was; he was exactly 51 years older than I. He lived to be 100, then terminated himself by refusing to eat or drink any more. If I live that long, I might follow his example. He was a historic radical who I understand was charged with treason, defended himself, and won. He was a smart, expressive man, and his kindnesses to our family helped us survive. For example, we had not known that you had to season wood before burning it in the wood burning stone. One day he drove in unasked with a truck full of seasoned firewood. What a difference that made! But I am not aware of any influence on my writing; we were merely neighbours and friends. He wrote about self-sufficient country life; I wrote science fiction and fantasy. He took steps to see that he never got rich; I became a millionaire. He was an arch leftist radical; I am an expressive liberal agnostic but not in his ball park.

You have written a large number of books, but I want to concentrate on the Xanth series. What gave you the idea to write these books?

Yes, I have published nearly 200 books. Xanth is special in more than one way. I mentioned getting blacklisted. After six years the publisher sent me a brochure, inviting me to submit material to them. I wrote back "Don't you know you're blacklisting me?" They wrote back that things had changed, and they had a notion of my situation. Indeed they did! Editor Lester del Rey had written for that publisher before, and when he became an editor there, he looked up his own figures, and discovered that while he had been credited with 69,000 sales for his novel, the actual figure was 169,000. So, he knew that my protest had been valid. I still think it is a shame that SFWA (the Science Fiction and Fantasy Writers of America), many of whose members were getting similarly cheated, supported that publisher and the blacklist. I once thought that writers were superior ethically; obviously not. Anyway, I wrestled with my conscience about whether to return to that publisher, and finally concluded that as it was under n'e w auspices, I should give it a chance. That, in retrospect, turned out to be the best decision of my career; they put me on the bestseller list, making me a name writer instead of a no-name writer. So, I worked out a fantasy novel, because that was the genre they wanted. That was "A Spell for Chameleon", the first Xanth novel. But I found I could not take fantasy seriously, so the humour and puns came in.

Is it difficult to write in a more simplistic for children without being too obvious?

I had no problem. In fact, the editor worried that the first Xanth novel would be taken as juvenile literature, so I upgraded the language. For example, instead of "high place" I used "lofty promontory." But children loved it anyway. Decades later I made a simplified language version, and they used that for the electronic edition.

The idea for each person to have a specific magical talent is a great one and a good plot mechanic. What gave you the idea? Were there any talents that you thought of that you had better not use because of the target age group of the books?

I don't remember, more than 40 years later, exactly how I came to think of having a magic talent for every person, but it does seem to have been a good idea. I think I just wanted our hero to be different from others, and in trouble because of it—the way I have been different all my life, and

often in trouble. The blacklisting is not the only example; I was suspended for a week in college because I stood my ground on a matter of principle, and was removed as an instructor, denied promotion, and put to weed pulling in the US Army for similar reason. Today I am the only one who will talk about those events; I think the others know they were wrong throughout. In Xanth, Bink was not without a magic talent; it simply wasn't an obvious one. Many readers seem to relate to that.

Puns are quite prominent in the books, particularly the magical plants such as the "Pan Trees" and so on – are you one of those guys that tells really terrible jokes at parties on purpose just to torture the other guests? (I mean this question in good fun)

No, in person I'm pretty conventional. Most of the puns now come from my readers. So, in answer to the question commonly asked of writers, where do their ideas come from, I answer "From my readers."

Did you base any of the characters in the books on real people?

Only a few. Jenny Elf is based on my correspondent Jenny, paralysed for life by a drunk driver. Good Magician Humfrey sort of parallels editor Lester Del Rey; and his wife, publisher Judy-Lynn del Rey identified with the Gorgon. The Gorgon is an attractive woman with one liability, a gaze that turns people to stone, who asked the Good Magician if he would marry her, and he made her serve a year's labour before giving her his answer. He was set in his ways. Some real people are minor characters who came to Xanth after their deaths, by the request of their friends or relatives. So, if you're not dead, don't ask. Most characters I simply make up. Once I parodied myself. I got accused of being an ogre at conventions, when I had never even attended a convention; critics are not much for accuracy. That annoyed me, so I made an ogre the hero of the next Xanth novel,"Ogre Ogre". which became my first national bestseller. After that I didn't mind being called an ogre; ogres are justly known for their stupidity.

There is a real- life conspiracy to keep fun things from children – how is this mirrored in the Xanth books?

That is exactly it. Xanth openly parodies the foolishness of the mundane realm. Some critics think that means I endorse sexism, but I parody it.

Are there any landmarks in Xanth that are based on real world ones? Obviously, things like the "keys" relate to the Florida Keys? I'm especially curious about "The Gap" – was this a real place that you knew?

We live beside the Withlacoochee River, which is "With- a- Cookee" in Xanth.

Tsala Apopka on the Florida map is associated with Lake Tsoda Popka. There's also the Kissimmee River, becoming the very friendly Kiss Mee; the Demon Corps of Engineers took hold of the two S's and pulled them straight, so it became the Kill Mee River, referring to the disastrous channelizing of the real river. There's Lake Ogre Chobee, and the Ogre fen Ogre Swamp. There's the Gold Coast, made of literal gold in Xanth. There's No Name Key, which actually exists, though you'll never find its secret access to Xanth. But the Gap Chasm differs. We bought forest property next to old railroad tracks that cut through a hill, so I exaggerated that small chasm effect and put it across central Xanth as the Gap Chasm. There actually is a fault buried below there, but it's not visible. Why doesn't it show on mundane maps? Because of the Forget Spell, naturally. Everything makes magical sense.

There are various plot themes that span the books – did you make it up as you went, or did you have an initial idea of how the inter-book plots would evolve?

I developed them through need. Originally, I thought Xanth would be a single novel. Obviously, I underestimated it.

Did you originally intend to make the series so extensive? It is over 40 books now so what keeps you going?

There are now 44 novels--the last three have not yet been published—and I am making notes for number 45 next year. For years or decades all publishers wanted from me was Xanth, and I am a commercial writer, so I wrote Xanths to pay my way. My more serious works are generally

ignored, like my ambitious Geodyssey historical series and my best fantasy, the ChroMagic series. I keep going because I love to write. Xanth is easy, it's fun, and it pays well, so that keeps it going.

Are there any books that you'd wish you'd written differently?

No, I am generally satisfied with what I have written. Some, like "Tarot", get chopped up by publishers. That was a quarter of a million-word novel, not three parts.

How's life now? Are you happy? What are you up to these days?

I am doing okay, considering that in August I will be 84. I still exercise, and read, and watch videos—I am going through the entire Star Trek series, hundreds of episodes, and am currently enjoying Deep Space Nine. My wife and I have been married 62 years, but her health is fragile, so we don't travel and tend to keep to ourselves. And of course, I am still writing; that's what I do. I will never retire from that.

Could there be a film or TV Series in the works? Do you know much about these – How involved are you?

There have been numerous movie or TV options, but none have worked out so far. I'm sure there will be a Xanth movie; I'd just like to see it happen while I am alive to appreciate it. My agent is checking out prospects; I am really not involved, apart from writing the novels. A movie or TV series would make me famous again, which would be nice, but that seems to be largely a matter of chance.

BLAKES 7

Blake's 7 was the "Dirty Dozen" in space, at a time when Star Trek was attempting to convert the universe to a politically correct nightmare – Blake's 7 was showing a more human side to the future – a darker and grittier one. Although Blake himself (played by Gareth Thomas) was a bit of a "goodie two-shoes" – his crew were a bunch of criminal misfits that were only together because it was safer that way. And when Blake was killed off early into the story, and Avon took over the leadership mantle, things turned even more interesting...

Paul
Darrow

Paul played Avon, the ruthless but charismatic leader of the group. He was good-looking, intelligent, but you couldn't trust him. Just the sort of anti-hero that I aspired to as a kid!

What prompted you to become an actor?

I've been asked this on a number of occasions. I always wanted to be a film producer and director. When I was young, I was told off actually because I spent more time in the cinema than anywhere else. I would see the various companies; there was one in particular called Hecht-Hill-Lancaster. Ben Hecht was a writer, Hill was a director, and Lancaster was Burt Lancaster, the actor and a big star.

I thought to myself, "Yes of course, that's very sensible. In order to become a producer director, you've got to deal with actors." When you are directing an actor saying, "I want you to do this," you've got to give him or her a reason. If you've been an actor yourself, then you're going to know what reason is. I thought, "I'll become an actor and then I'll become a director and a producer." Then I did a little bit of directing later on and producing, but very little came of it, so I just became an actor. It continued from there and I enjoyed it.

I went to Royal Academy of Dramatic Art. RADA. It was fascinating. They teach you all sorts of things; they help you with your voice projection and movement. I learned how to fence, how to dance in various styles because you sometimes have to dance in a play, do a tango or something like that. I was a pretty good dancer but I have since lost my legs. I'm confined to a wheelchair now so I only do audio work really now, although I am in an episode of Pointless the quiz. RADA taught me a lot and I progressed from there.

How did you get your first break into television?

I was on tour with a play called Chips With Everything by Sir Arnold Wesker. Arnold had written this wonderful play and I did the touring version. We played in Manchester and Granada TV showed it as a television series. Sarah Lawson and Edwin Richfield were the stars.

Edwin was very pleasant and so was Sarah Lawson, who was married, I believe, to Patrick Allen with whom I later worked. They asked me to do it and it was a small part. I got paid £100, which in 1962-3, was a lot of money so I decided to do it. Curiously enough, there was another actor, a Canadian who'd been over here, and he had a small part in it and that was Donald Sutherland.

In those days, there were a lot of repertory theatres all around the country. I knew actors/actresses who didn't do anything else; they went from repertory company to repertory company throughout the year. They would do three months in York and then they'd go off to Blackpool or over to Liverpool or down to Weston-Super-Mare.

You would undoubtedly be seen at some town and another by someone and they would say, "How about doing this show?" so I would end up doing some TV such as Emergency Ward 10. Back in the day, I did quite a lot on Carlton TV, Granada and ITV. I did an episode of The Saint with Roger Moore and I really enjoyed that.

How was the role of Avon sold to you?

It was quite a good idea. I got it from Terry Nation who also wrote Dr Who. I became very good friends and part of his family really. He told me he pitched it as Robin Hood and or The Dirty Dozen in outer space. I don't think you'll find a hero who is such a nasty piece of work as Avon. He was an anti-hero, if you like. I think Terry pretty much created that character; the bad guy who is your hero. I remember the guests on the show were saying that they'd never been in a show where the hero is such a bastard.

Realistically, Avon was the more identifiable character because at that time, even the baddies would tell people to turn around, so they can shoot them. Why would people give them a chance to escape like that? Avon would happily shoot people in the back, and that appealed to the viewers. He was, as it were, more realistic.

Also, he wore good costumes. I was also allowed to get away with cool remarks which were a bit risky at the time. People found that quite amusing. I remember talking to Gareth Thomas, who played Blake for two seasons. I said, "You appeal to all the young school children, school lads. And I appeal to 40-year-old divorcees" Gareth laughed at that and said, "Yes, I think you're right."

Were you interested in science fiction?

No, no interest whatsoever. I didn't know what it was talking about half the time. I was lucky enough to be able to go to conventions all over America. In New York, I met Isaac Asimov. Isaac and I were chatting and he said to me with a deep voice, "Have you ever read any science fiction?" I said, "No, not really." He said, "Well, you might start by reading my books." I said, "Yes, all right." So I read a couple of Isaac Asimov's and that was really my introduction to proper science fiction. He was a very clever man and, although I only met him at that one convention, he was very pleasant.

Were there any instances where you thought Avon was made to act in the way that was unrealistic to the character?

Yes, many times. Particularly after Gareth left. I remember in the first episode of series three I had a fight scene with a very good stunt man, also called Gareth. Gareth made me look really good because I threw him over my shoulder. I didn't really. I just put my shoulder there and he threw himself over it. It was great.

He was flat on the floor and then Simon, who was a new character, said to me, "I'll kill him." Avon said, "No, leave him." Which didn't seem part of Avon's character to me. I said to the producer, "He wouldn't ever have done that, he would have just said, "'Yes, go ahead. You either do it or I will." The producer said, "No, we want to soften him a bit, because, he's now the leader of the pack." Sometimes it went against the grain.

The science fiction shows of the era were quite low budget. Did you have any problems with failing props or that sort of thing?

I used to be known as the breaker of guns because they were plastic and I used to break them. I used to drop them, and pieces would fall off. In the end, they made me one with an aluminium core so that it wouldn't break, and somebody nicked it. Typical! Then, when we got to the fourth season, they pushed the boat out a bit, and we had proper hand guns which made a noise; a bit of a whizzing sound. You get a bang so you know the thing has actually fired.

The show was quite brave in the sense it seemed to have no qualms about killing off the major characters.

That was Terry's idea to kill off a major character in the early stages. Although he told me later on that they had said, "Should we kill off the Avon character?" He said, "No way." He wouldn't allow that. He admitted afterwards that Avon was his favourite and he liked what I did with the role.

I think the surprising plot twists certainly helped. I think a lot of the success for Blake's 7 was to do with the chemistry of the characters and the actors who played them. I remember asking a producer at one point if the casting was calculated or just a bit of good luck? He said, "Of course, it's perfect casting."

The show when it finally ended, do you think it had come to its proper end or do you think there was more scope?

No. I thought it would be longer – in America, for example, Star Trek had a five-year mission so that told you that there were going to be five seasons. So, I thought that if you want to sell the series in America, you need five seasons. I thought there'd be one more, but there wasn't. Although Terry wanted to do a mini-series afterwards because they were quite fashionable at the time.

I know there's a been a lot of talk of reviving the series.

Yes, there was a lot of talk of that over the years, and I was often involved with it as a kind of figure head I suppose, but it never came to anything. It's a shame, but these things happen. Time passed and we move on. Big Finish audio books have continued the stories of Blakes 7 and they use the original actors to voice them where possible, and I've worked on a few of those titles myself.

Was there anything you'd change if you had your career again?

Yes, I would change an awful lot of things knowing what I know now. I'd like to start my life all over again knowing what I know now. I would have stuck to what I originally wanted to do which was to be a producer, director and actor. I would have ended up like Clint Eastwood, who acts, directs and produces movies and works with people that he wants to work with like Gene Hackman.

I've never worked with him but I know some people who have, and they said he's wonderful because it's all just so cool and laid back. You just get on with it and it's enjoyable. He just goes into bringing the actor in and Gene Hackman might say, "Was I in the right place?" He goes, "Yes I think so. Do you want to do it again?" You trust him and you say, "No okay fine." The film comes in on budget and in time. He's great to work with.

So that's what I would do and still be an actor, then move to the production and direction area.

Are you still in touch with anyone from the cast of Blake's 7?

Yes. Jan Chappell, who played Cally. She called me the other day, and we had a long talk on how things are going. I speak to Steven Pacey, who played Tarrant quite often too. Michael Keating is a regular guest – he pops over for a few drinks and stays over. I'm lucky in that the cast got on so very well in the series that we've remained friends ever since.

DARK STAR

The film is a Science Fiction low budget movie (estimated at around $60,000) made whilst at film college by legendary director John Carpenter in 1974.

A small crew pilot a slowly deteriorating spaceship (Dark Star) with an important mission – to destroy unstable planets in otherwise habitable star systems to prepare for future colonisation. Each of the four remaining crew members (the captain died prior to the film's beginning) have become alienated from each other, and fight boredom as well as each other.

There is Lieutenant Doolittle who dreams of being on a beach surfing all day, who can barely tolerate the others - particularly the childish Sergeant Pinback, the bombardier that plays practical jokes on everyone else. Talby the target specialist remains in his observation deck and won't mix with the others and Corporal Boiler the navigator, who has turned a little bit psychotic and plays with the emergency guns for fun.

Whilst the darker side of loneliness is explored, the film is by far the funniest Sci Fi film I've ever seen too – Pinback's battle with the beachball alien being a high point of the movie.

Brian Narelle

Brian played Lieutenant Doolittle (in his only film role, and had to contend with often dangerous filming conditions – there is little wonder he captured Doolittle's resigned demeanour.

How did you get the role in Dark Star?

I shared a house with John Carpenter and others. We were all at USC (University of South California) film school together. John, one day, walked in to the room and said, "Will you be in my next film?" He took me out to lunch and said, "I want to make you a movie star", I said, "What the hell are you talking about?". Then he explained how we were going to go uptown and film this short film he had written called "Dark Star"! And lo and behold that's what happened. The university was not happy about that though, because he was basically using university equipment to film it all. I avoided going back to USC for a while because I was involved, and I thought I might be thought guilty by association.

How did John sell the concept of Dark Star to you?

John had just won the Academy Award for students - The way it worked back then was that they used to have a Student's Oscar as part of the big ceremony on TV. John Carpenter had worked on a film as a student, and it had been nominated. We were all in the shared house watching the ceremony in the kitchen, and John was watching it in his bedroom with his girlfriend. It got to the time for the winner of the student academy awards "...and the winner is "The Resurrection of Broncho Billy". It was directed by one of John's friends, but John did the editing, co-writing and the soundtrack for it. We were jumping up and down because John just won an Oscar! John came out of his bedroom to grab a coke out of the fridge and I shook his hand and I congratulated him, and he went back in his bedroom.

John and Dan just came up with the idea for Dark Star, and at college we always helped with each other's projects. And you don't turn down an Oscar winner! It took over three years to make in total, on and off. Every time he had enough money to do more filming, we got together. My understanding is that he and Dan O'Bannon (Dan co-wrote Dark Star, did the special effects and starred as "Pinback"), took their tuition money and they used it to buy film instead of paying the school. I don't think they ever got their degrees because they weren't attending classes, but I don't think they cared! John had his own way of doing things.

At the start of the filming, I'd organised a little gathering at one point because I wanted to do some improvisation and explore the characters. It became very clear early in that meeting, that John and Dan didn't have any interest in that and all they wanted us to do was "show up and do what we tell you". Then we started filming it. Dan had built the space ship control room in the south stage of the school film department. Dan did almost all of the set building out of old pieces of junk.

My control panel had illuminated buttons that were backlit upside-down plastic ice cube trays. I was at my girlfriend's house, when she bought a new Sony TV. It was a little one, but it came in a big box full of Styrofoam. She was about to throw the packaging away. I took it and I just gave it to Dan, who was brilliant at turning junk into a film set. I forgot all about it and I never saw it again until the world premiere on Hollywood Boulevard in '74! Talby entered the airlock in his spacesuit and the back of his spacesuit has these big white things. That was the packing from my girlfriend's TV set!

The Bomb (#20) was made from a model kit of a trailer truck. It's the back of an 18-wheeler. It's got pieces of model battleship stuck all over it to make it look "spacey". The model was about 12-inches long. But if you look at the scale of the bomb model to the spaceship model you can tell that there is no-way you could fit 20 of them in there! That's one of the things that made it funny.

There was a list a year or two ago on Facebook for the 10 films you need to see to learn to make movies. It included some classics like "Citizen Cane" and some basic stuff as you can imagine. It also included "Dark Star" among the 10 films you need to see. The reason it was on the list was because if you don't have any money and you're using that for an excuse then forget it because those guys did it with nothing. The whole film including special effects and the optical blow up to 35 millimetres from 16 was $60,000. I've worked on some TV series and movies recently and I'm sure the budget for the food for one day was more than that. I was out working on a Marvel movie recently at six in the morning and we were having lunch. It's crazy because I looked around the room and 300 people in the room eating very well and they were only the second unit doing parts like stunt driving scenes.

Did you get paid for being in "Dark Star"?

I got totally screwed on the payments for the film; I didn't get paid a cent. One day John presented all of us with our contracts and release forms. He said, "You need to sign all this stuff so that the film can be released." It mentioned the percentages we would receive. Everybody else just scribbled and signed it, I said, "I want to show this to my attorney." That annoyed John but what could he do?

My attorney looked over the contract and he said, "This doesn't make any sense", and told me not to sign it. I went back to John and I said, "On the advice of my attorney, I'm not signing this." Then later on I noticed that the film got released anyway! Basically, I got paid nothing. The only money I received for it was two years ago. The BBC did a three-part series on "The History of Sci-Fi" and under SAG contract rules they paid me a chunk of money. So 40 years later was my first payment.

Dan lived in the same house as yourself and John. What was he like to live with?

Shall we say a "loose cannon"? One day there was a really loud, noisy car that was going up and down the street. I heard that he went out and started shooting at the car's tyres. Now, I wasn't there so I can't validate that, but I don't doubt it either.

I didn't live with Dan very long though. I lived with John much longer. There were about seven of us in that house and we had just moved there after finding a place in a gated community where ambassadors lived. We lived there for about five or six days before neighbours figured out that these film students had just occupied a mansion. They had us thrown out in about a week. Then we found a house up in the Hollywood Hills and seven of us moved into there.

Did anything go wrong in filming Dark Star that was kept in the Movie?

The scene in "Dark Star" when Boiler takes out that knife and starts doing that stabby thing between his own fingers. I can barely stand to watch it now. He actually stabbed his finger! He was a trooper though; he just kept going. I watched his finger turn white and I saw blood everywhere. The sound of the knife going in was really horrible. People might think that's a fake finger but it is not a fake finger. You can't really hear the sound that I actually heard. I can still remember it, so it bothers me.

Tell us about the freezer scene.

We were meant to do that part of the film in November and the shoot kept expanding and getting a life of its own – it was going on for two or three years. By the summer, I was walking across campus and I saw my acting buddies and a theatre professor sitting on a bench. I just plopped down with them just to say hello. The professor turns to me, he says, " Want to go to Europe?" and I looked at him like, "Who's paying for this?" He says, "We are."

I informed Dan and John that I was leaving for a few weeks. They hadn't done the freezer scene yet and they had to throw the freezer scene together really fast and they were very unhappy with me that I had the audacity to have a life of my own. I have no idea if the kerosene mist was vengeful or just all they could get their hands on but do not try acting in kerosene mist because it is toxic stuff.

At the beginning of the scene I'm coming down a ladder into a small area that is full of literally poisonous mist. Before we filmed each "take", I had a wet face cloth pressed to my face. Every time John yelled "action!" I would just throw the face cloth away and turn around and do a take on that scene. It's nasty stuff; it's also very slippery so I could have just slipped on my ass at any moment. We only took a break when Carpenter couldn't take it anymore behind the camera.

We were shooting 16 millimetre in those days in colour and it takes a hell of a lot of lighting to look right, so it's also really hot. There was another problem with the space suit - another breathing problem that they hadn't thought of ahead of time. As soon as they put the helmet on me under those lights, it immediately fogged up because there's no ventilation. Dan found some plastic tubing and stuck it in my mouth. It was awkward to move. He often ripped the helmet off my head after filming, which would then take my ears with it. That really, really hurt; it was torture.

I was in a film production of Shakespeare's Henry V, and I was offered two roles – either King Henry's uncle or the Archbishop of Canterbury. My experiences of "Dark Star" have haunted me. I actually chose the Archbishop of Canterbury for totally practical reasons. As King Henry's uncle, I pictured myself on a real horse in the woods freezing to death with a sword, and then maybe falling off or getting hit by a weapon. I wound up as the Archbishop of Canterbury because it's almost entirely safe; I didn't fall off any horses and I didn't get whacked by a sword. After a while, you start to think practically.

You are a frustrated surfer in the film. Are you a surfer in real life?

I was indeed that in the film. In fact, Jack Harris, one of the producers on "Dark Star", wanted some flashback scenes of me on the beach being a surfer with some bikini babes in and running down the beach and John said, "No way. Not doing that." John won that battle. So I never got so sit on a beach with the bikini babes.

In reality, I've been up on a surfboard once and I fell off immediately. I do love to body surf but standing up on a board didn't work out so well. When "Dark Star" made its rounds in Australia, it was a big hit among surfers; they liked that.

When was the last time you spoke to John? Are you still in touch with him?

When he was filming "Village of the Damned", (the remake). He filmed that up here in Northern California. I knew he was filming but I didn't know where. I actually just drove around West County and I saw the film tracks. I just pulled in and I walked in past

security. They didn't see me. Finally, somebody saw me and said, "Who are you? What are you doing here?" I explained who I was. They said, "John's wife is going to be here in a minute."

His wife pulled in. She said, "Hi Brian - Hop in the car. I'll take you out to location." She drove me out into the fields where they had a lot of these fake dead cows. John walked up to the car, and the last thing he expected to see was me, so that took him aback. He asked if I was still in the business. I told him that I have a couple of Emmys but because I didn't have the Hollywood cred that he had; he was sort of dismissive, I felt.

In terms of John, those were the very brief encounters I said. "I hope maybe we could catch up at the convention and have a beer or something." I gave him my number but he never called. It feels like he has put "Dark Star" behind him.

Over the years, it wasn't just called "Dark Star" anymore. It became "John Carpenter's Dark Star" or "John Carpenter's The Thing" or "John Carpenter's Escape from New York". It's always his name above the title. Dan had so much to do with co-writing "Dark Star", designing it, special effecting it, and even co-starring in it He edited it too and when I see this "John Carpenter's Dark Star," it feels like that's not true.

I did a cartoon for Diane O'Bannon (Dan's wife) after Dan had died. It was a marquee of a movie theatre. It said, "John Carpenter's Dark Star" in the marquee. I'm walking away on the side walk with the step ladder, having just hung series of signs over the big official sign outside.

It said "John Carpenter's Dark Star co-written by Dan O'Bannon, co-starring Dan O'Bannon, special effects by Dan O'Bannon, edited by Dan O'Bannon". It felt like I needed to say, "Better late than never. Let's give him some credit here."

Were you quite surprised at the success of the film?

Absolutely! Because it took so long to happen! When the film premiered, no one laughed. No one realised it was supposed to be a comedy. I think that hurt Dan the most. Dan said, "If I can't make them laugh, I'll scare all the shit out of them." And that's where the film "Alien" came from!

"Dark Star" fans are everywhere, and they sometimes track me down too. A few months ago, I got home and there was a package on my front door. There was a big box. I sometimes order stuff from Amazon so I was thinking, "What the hell did I order and why?" I opened it. I hadn't ordered it at all. It was a gift from a "Dark Star" fan. He had replicated my helmet completely right down to the numbers, details and writing; everything about it. He just did that as a gift and sent it to me. I was stunned!

Online, I discovered a model maker, who makes all kinds of real NASA and also "Star Trek" and "Battlestar Galactica". He actually makes a "Dark Star" model. You have to put it together, but it's made up of resin, not plastic. I wrote to him, because he's in Cornwall. He had a price on it in UK pounds, but I had no idea how to translate the money and the shipping costs. I didn't know what to do so I wrote to him and I asked him. He said, "You're not paying for it," and he sent it to me. I put it together and I still have it. There's nothing left of that film. There's no swag; there's no memorabilia. The only thing that I was aware of that was taken from the set was Bomb #20 which my friend Dale Dalton had. He worked on the film as an editor. He lives down on the beach near where I live. He told me that, at one point, he had it on the shelf in his apartment. Then there was an earthquake and it fell off the shelf and broke. He just threw it away; he didn't fix it. He just threw it away, but I have a model of the ship and I have my helmet.

After "Dark Star", how did your life pan out?

Well, I started cartooning when I was eight years old. I was published when I was about 13. Then I wound up obviously going to film school, and I was acting there too. When acting and cartooning and film school get together, you wind up falling into animation. It just happens to you.

Right after school, John Carpenter went on to make "The Thing", and Dan O'Bannon went on to make "Alien", and another guy we lived with, Terry Winkless, wrote "The Howling" and I went directly to writing for "Sesame Street"! So they were dealing with monsters and I had a certain relationship with Cookie Monster.

How did you get the job writing for Sesame Street?

My girlfriend's best friend's boyfriend was a producer in Hollywood, and he was connected to animation studio and they were solicited to do some stuff for Sesame Street. So he passed it on to me and I was paid a little bit of money to come up with some stuff. I was up all night the night before I turned it in, anguishing over this material, and I thought what I had written was pure crap.

I really didn't want to turn it in I actually wouldn't have except he'd already paid me, so I had to. I grudgingly turned it in, and he looked it over and he said, "You're going to make a lot of money in this town kid". Out of the six scripts that I turned in, Sesame Street bought half of them. That was the beginning of my relationship with Sesame Street. I'm also a puppeteer, so I've done many puppet shows for kids and TV series for Discovery and I produced in New Zealand. I'm all over the map.

I've written dozens of films for Paramount and Sammy Schuster for children dealing with issues like sexual abuse and alcoholism, but for little kids and understanding AIDS. These were mostly done with puppets. I have 11 films where I'm a puppy dog and there are other films where I'm a dragon, a fish, and a bunny rabbit. Then my wife and I co-starred in a series she created called "Bingo & Molly", where we're bunny rabbits and

I am also a wolf. At one point I was supervising animator and sequence director with Lucasfilm, and Warner Bros. on an animated feature.

I was so frustrated by the amount of effort it takes to create an animated feature; it put me off my cartoon and animation work. I started to get heavily into puppets because you can achieve something on film very fast with puppets that would take you months or years to do in animation. So that's when I switched camp.

I wound up writing a short animated film called "Hubert's Brain" that won the Annie Award in 2001, which is the Oscars of animation. It was computer animated and I merely wrote it, I didn't animate it. So I stepped out of the trenches and took on more of a writing role and I've been doing that ever since.

DELIVERANCE

Deliverance is a film about an ill-fated canoe trip taken by four ordinary guys. Set against stunning scenes of rapids, Cajun woodlands and hostile red-necks, it is a story of friendship, and redemption. There are also two or three classic scenes that have been referenced heavily in all forms of media – the "Squeal like a pig" scene, and of course "Duelling Banjos" scene in particular.

Ronnie Cox

Ronnie Cox played the mild-mannered Drew Ballinger in the film, in his first ever movie role. He was the only member of the group not to survive (although the other members had a pretty rough time of it too). Ronnie later had prominent roles in Robocop, Total Recall, and Beverly Hills Cop.

How was your home life as a child? It was quite a rural area I believe?

I grew up in a little village called Cloudcroft, New Mexico. I'm the middle child of five kids. I just grew up with the lower middle-class people. My dad was a truck driver, and then a carpenter and a maintenance man. There you have it. They were a pretty uneducated family. I'm one of the first people on either side of my family ever to go to college, much less graduate. It was largely a family that grew up without books, really. Although my dad did play guitar, but he played for square dances and stuff like that.

Your first role was notable for your guitar playing. And you can play in real life too. Was it your dad that taught you to play?

A little, but we lived in an area that was known for its music. 19 miles north of where we lived is Clovis, New Mexico, which in the late '50s and early '60s was a hotbed of recording. It's not generally known but I was actually at the recording session when Buddy Holly cut Peggy Sue. There were a lot of artists,

Sugar Shack, or the Fireballs, and Jimmie Dale Gilmore, and people like that. They were all cutting records there.

When I was in high school, Norman Petty of Norman Petty Studios, which is where all those things were cut, noticed a singing group I was in at an exchange assembly and hired us to sing backup on some record for a girl named Hope Griffin. I was singing backup on these records when I was in high school.

I also had a rock and roll band back in those days. Rob's Rock Out. Three of us in the band were

brothers. My older brother, Rick, was my bass player and I was the leader of the band - the lead singer, and then my younger brother, Mike, was the lead guitarist.

But I knew my whole life I just wanted to be an actor I mainly grew up watching old western movies. Gene Autry, Roy Rogers, those kinds of films. No great artistic films really... Then I saw The Treasure of the Sierra Madre when I was about 12 or 13 years old and from that moment on, I knew that I wanted to be an actor. The Treasure of the Sierra Madre was just so different from those because all of a sudden, I was seeing a quality movie instead of a B-Western.

Were your family supportive of your new ambitions?

No, actually after I went to college, they always thought I was throwing my life away to get educated and then to become an actor. They thought it was a total waste of time and effort.

What were your first breaks into acting?

Well, when I was in college, there was an acting company

up in Colorado that I joined. It was $20 a week with room and board. I'd go up and do old-time melodramas at this tourist town.

When we left college, my wife Mary and I went back east. Mary is a brilliant woman, and she had a National Science Foundation fellowship at Georgetown University. She was working on her Ph.D. in chemistry and I started to work at a place in Washington DC called Arena Stage. It's considered one of the finest theatres in America outside of New York. I went there as what they euphemistically call a "production intern2, which was basically a glorified word for "slave".

I then became an assistant stage manager and occasionally got to play little tiny parts in plays. We were there in Washington DC for six years and basically, at the end of that time, I could read a script and knew my way around a stage. If I was getting any parts though it would be the smallest role in the play. Mary then got her Ph.D, so we went to New York and I managed to get a bit part in a Broadway show. That's when John Boorman came to New York looking for good unknown actors to star in Deliverance, and God knows I was definitely unknown! I had been a struggling actor for about 10 or 11 years by then.

How did your first meeting with John go?

Well, actually I was the first actor they saw in New York. The reason I was the first actor they saw was not because I was the top of anyone's list, but because I was the bottom of the list. They were going to start seeing people at 10 o'clock in the morning on a Sunday. They asked me to come at nine o'clock just to see if I was actually worth seeing. I met with the casting director, and he gave

me a copy of the script and told me to go away to a coffee shop and come back later. Then I came back later, and met with John Boorman. I ended up meeting with John two or three more times during that week. I have to tell you the truth, the fact that I could play guitar was also instrumental, (pun intended) in getting that far in the interview process.

Eventually, they flew a bunch of us from New York out here to California and screen tested us for the four roles. They tested about 15 or 16 of us. I was the only one that they liked out of the whole group I was in. Then a couple of weeks later, they were still looking for people, and they found Ned Beatty in Washington DC. It's probably the first time in the history of film that the two guys below the title were cast before the two guys above the title. They obviously decided that Burt and Jon were going to play the lead roles.

Was it quite daunting being in a film with Burt Reynolds and Jon Voight?

You've got to realize that at that time Burt Reynolds wasn't a big star, and he was a television actor. If you were a television actor in those days, you were considered a cut or two below film actors. So, in many ways, Deliverance was as big a breakthrough for Burt as it was for myself and Ned (being our first film).

Jon Voight, of course, had done Midnight Cowboy the year before so, he was on his way up, but otherwise we as a group were what John Boorman wanted. Not established film actors.

What struck you immediately when you started to film Deliverance?

In many ways, since it was my first film and my first time in front of a camera, it was hard to remember that we were making a film because it was just a bunch of people playing boy scouts.

And the thing about Deliverance that most people don't realize, was that we shot the film in chronological sequence. It had never happened before as far as I am aware. We had to do it that way because we were travelling throughout the story and couldn't head back to previous locations easily. We were travelling downstream in canoes and back tracking would have been almost impossible. Incidentally, we did all the canoeing ourselves, there's no stuntmen. All four of us are really pretty good athletes, and we had two weeks of canoeing practice before we started. Which was a good job because in the film, the rapids get harder and harder as we went along. By the time we got to the really hard rapids, the really difficult ones, we've all been on the water for six or eight hours a day for five or six or eight weeks. We all pretty much knew what we were doing.

Jon Voight and I, we were in a wooded "Old Town" canoe, which is not even intended for whitewater. It's a lake canoe, and because of that, we capsized a lot. We wrecked six or seven canoes in total - in the film at the end when we found that canoe broken in half. We did that when we were actually canoeing. They didn't have to smash one in half. We did that ourselves, going over the rocks and rapids...

Did anyone actually get hurt?

Yes, we all did. Burt, he really messed up his hip pretty badly. I almost drowned once. Ned almost drowned once. We were lucky to come out in one piece. John's feeling about making a film was that if you were doing a shot that was so dangerous that you need a stuntman, then you probably shouldn't be doing that shot. He wanted realism. He didn't want a shot that only expert stuntmen could achieve. So, we did everything. Afterwards he realized how much we dodged the bullet and no one got seriously injured. There were a lot of things that could have gone wrong because we were down there with basically no way for anyone to help us if we got into trouble (except for the film crew). You'd be pretty much on your own a lot of the time.

There are a few iconic scenes in the film - Dueling Banjos being one of them. What are your recollections?

We shot it for two or three days. Because first of all, neither Billy nor I were actually playing. Billy was the child that played the Banjo (except that he wasn't - that's another one of those myths). The song was pre-recorded by Eric Weisberg and Steve Mendell.

Billy didn't even know enough about the banjo to fake playing. We didn't even have real strings on the Banjo. He was sitting on a porch swing with his arm behind his back as tightly as he can get it. There's another little kid hiding behind Billy that knows something about the Banjo that has the same type of shirt on, that pretended to be Billy's his left arm, and he's reaching up and pretending to play, he's moving his fingers. I wish I had played on the soundtrack though, as that

would have earned me about a million dollars a year! That's a big scene. With all of the dancing and Jon and Burt and Ned and all the townspeople around. It took us a while to do it and it was the first

thing we shot in the movie. Here I am doing that big scene, my very first time in front of the camera.

The scene where they find your body, and you have a dislocated arm was a powerful scene. Did you wear a prosthetic arm?

No, I had polio when I was young and my shoulder can now pop out of place. That's actually me. When I got down to Georgia, the original concept that John Boorman wanted for when they find Drew drowned, he originally wanted them to find Drew being face up in the water with his eyes open. I was being fitted with false eyeballs. While they were doing that, I said to John Boorman, "You know, I can do a really weird thing

with my shoulder." I showed him and he almost fell down. I read a lot of people think that that was the worst prosthetic they've ever seen but it's just actually me.

Were you quite surprised at the success of the film?

Everybody knew that it was going to be a great film. Every major actor in the world wanted those four roles. We were nominated for an Academy Award that year. Of course, we were also in competition with The Godfather, so we weren't going to win. We all knew that this was special.

The problem was, for that time because of the homosexual rape, it was almost, especially in the south, kind of considered a porno movie. It freaked a lot of southern guys out, to say the truth. But what it did for both me and Ned was unbelievable. All of a sudden, I was being offered roles that I would never even have been offered before.

Did you think working in the theatre was a benefit to you?

Absolutely. Stage acting requires a whole lot of technique that you can master but there were a lot of techniques that weren't necessarily useful for film. I'll tell you something that you probably have never heard before - I'm one of the few actors who think that you have to be a much more accomplished actor to work on film and television than you do on stage. You can get away with a lot of tricks on stage, that you cannot get away with on film. Therefore, you can take any really good film actor as far as I'm concerned.

He might need some training about projecting and some of the technical aspects but he'll still be good on stage. Unfortunately, the opposite is not always true.

You could take a lot of fabulous stage actors and they're a positive embarrassment on film. I can give you a prime example. Sir Laurence Olivier may well have been one of the great stage actors of all time, but I can tell you, as a matter of fact, he's a positive embarrassment as a film actor. He's terrible. Go and see a film called The Betsy or see the production of Cat on a Hot Tin Roof with him playing Big Daddy. I've seen amateurs in junior high that could act better in films. Now having said that, I know I'm treading on the hallowed ground here... but there are other actors, such as Sir John Gielgud, who was a wonderful stage actor as well as a really, really great film actor.

Because here's the thing, if you're doing a stage show, and, say there are 1800 seats, no one past about the third or fourth row can see what's going on in your eyes. In film acting, when that camera comes in and it's close on that, there better be something going on behind your eyes. If it's nothing going on there then that's when you're just up there gesturing.

Was John easy to work for?

We largely improvised Deliverance. Although, I'm not implying at all that John Boorman wasn't in absolute total strict control of it. We had two weeks of rehearsal before that film started. We went through every scene, broke down every scene with the four of us and every one of us knew every line backwards and forwards. You were always free to say the line as you would there as long as it doesn't mess up the play and as long as it didn't mess

up your fellow actors. You always had that freedom. Then of course John Boorman would say either that worked out or didn't work and then you would go on from there. There was always a real collaborative feeling about that film. Although a collaborative with John Boorman being the arbiter of the collaboration.

In your earlier films you play quite laid-back characters but then after a while, you started to play really evil authoritarian businessmen types, such as your role in RoboCop?

Yes. I see in many ways, that was the thing, especially back in those days. They still do it certainly to an extent, sort of typecast. Since I played Drew, the sensitive moralistic one in Deliverance, for some reason if you played a character that had any sort of sensitivity usually got equated with weak. So, after Deliverance hit the screens, for about the next 10 years, I played Mr. Boy Scout, nice guy in films because I was known as this really nice actor. In many ways, RoboCop was as big a boon to my career as Deliverance was, because now all of a sudden, I got to play this new type of guy. Because there's been 10 years of residual goodwill built up from audiences, suddenly seeing my character in RoboCop develop into a nasty guy sort of shocked them – which is one of the reasons the film worked so well. Once I played Dick Jones, then I got offered everything. Then there was a period there for about five or six or eight years in the eighties and nineties where I seemed to be in every film made.

Total Recall, The Onion Field, Taps, Murder at 1600. I've been really blessed that I've been in some really good quality films. Even Beverly Hills Cop...

Which one was your favourite film?

Let me ask you, do you have children? Which one is your favourite? You see what I mean? You can't really pick one, can you?

No, each film has its own needs and its own direction that you have to approach it from. It has to be interesting for me to act in if I take a role. I've always set out to be really selective about the films I do, but that's not to say that I don't do crap, it's just that I don't do crap on purpose.

The Hitch Hikers Guide to the Galaxy

he Hitchhikers' Guide to the Galaxy was something I originally grew to
e when I read the book. It was my first contact with Douglas Adam's
que way of storytelling and style of humour – a very clever humour
t used language gymnastics to creep a joke in when you were least
ecting it.

as over joyed when the BBC made a TV series. But by far the best part
he TV series (for me at least) were the amazing guide book entries –
wn as a series of animations (brilliantly voiced by Peter Jones), that
only kept the viewer informed of what was happening in the show, but
e so deliciously hilarious too...

Rod Lord

od Lord was the man responsible for bringing the Hitchhikers guide
ries to life – he has also worked on TV shows such as Terrahawks, and
x Headroom.

How did the Hitch Hikers Guide job come about?

We had a studio in Hanwell. It spanned half the ground floor of a little film company called Athos, called Athos House. BBC had cutting rooms in half of the ground floor, and we had the rest.

I had a fairly new young assistant who had just started working with us, called Kevin, who was mad about Science Fiction – programmes such as Dr. Who, Blake's 7, or anything in that vein including Star Wars. He heard some R2D2 sounds coming from down the corridor one day. He crept down there and he gathered from what he could hear that they were cutting for a BBC "Jim'll Fix it". A kid on the show had got to meet the Star Wars robot. My assistant-manager went to ingratiate himself with the people doing the editing. It was Alan Bell, who was the director/producer on what would become "Hitchhikers".

Alan was talking to my assistant and said, "I've just got a new job to start. I don't really know how or what to do with it. It's something called "Hitchhiker's Guide to the Galaxy". There's a lot of crap going to be involved and I don't quite know how to handle it because the BBC have said they can't do it with computer animation." The BBC had a brand-new computer department at the time but they said it wasn't a practical project to undertake for them.

Kevin invited him to come and have a look at our show reel because he thought we could do something to help. Alan came along with Kevin and we had a look. Alan brought Douglas Adams, the author of Hitchhikers Guide to the Galaxy, back to have a look. They were quite enthusiastic and asked us to do a test piece to see if it will work. The piece they gave us as out trial piece was the first half of "Babel fish". When they saw that, they decided that it looked like it might work.

We had a really good liaison guy called Doug Burd. He was a BBC guy who was a designer and he sat with us all throughout production. He was very good. So that's how it came about. It was by complete chance and it was one of the most enjoyable jobs we ever had to do.

I think the Babel fish was probably my favourite animation from the series.

It's certainly the best known. It's ripped off all over the place of course; there are online translators and all sorts of stuff that have used the name and graphics style. I've stopped trying to take Babel fish images off the internet because it's an impossible task. People have mouse mats, t-shirts, mugs, and goodness knows what else. It's a loser's game, so I've given up really. It was ground-breaking stuff at the time. Did you use any effects software were to create any of it or was it literally just hand-animated?

It was all completely handcrafted. The funny thing was after the first episode went out, we had a phone call from a computer magazine. It was saying they wanted to know whether we've actually used the new Sinclair flat screen to generate this stuff electronically. We had to say no and explain that there was lots of hand labour involved. There was nothing electronic about it at all; it was completely handcrafted. We did it by multiple camera passes; sometimes up to 12, 14, or 16 runs so it was all done in motion camera. It was backlit and we did multiple passes to achieve where it was difficult to get multiple colours by cutting backlit channels.

After three or four days of shooting, you would look at the rushes and go, "Oh God. We've got to start again. A hair in the gate!" Those were the drawbacks and that method of doing it was very time-consuming, a very clunky way of doing it.

In the end, we generated about 45 minutes' worth of screen-time including the 35 minutes for the "Heart of Gold" spaceship sequences. We did actually buy a computer and had learnt how to use it. We were hoping to use it for the second series of Hitchhikers, which in theory, there was going to be.

Unfortunately, Douglas decided to go to Hollywood at that point. The call from the BBC saying, "Sorry guys. It's been pulled." came two weeks before we were due to start episode one. That was a bit of a traumatic time, really. We've just spent about £75000 on our first computer which was fridge sized and needed an air-conditioned room. Luckily, we did manage to get our work through it so in the end it worked out all right. We managed to get some work in advertising, commercials - that sort of thing.

One thing I loved about the Hitchhiker's animations - it has a retro-modern style.

Probably you're assuming that it might have been a more conscious design achievement than it probably was. A lot of it was

accidental. It was down to what was possible in the time by doing tricks under the camera just to save time and that saved the amount of artwork that had to be cloned. What you're describing is something that

probably was not articulated in our minds when we were doing it. A lot of it was just a serendipitous result of practicalities of what was possible at the time and the money available and all that. That's it really.

Were there any animations in HitchHikers that you had to alter in a way that you didn't agree with?

In the early days, the very first Babel fish designs that I came up with were quite cartoony. They were going to be conventional cartoon animations in a way, but

they were going to be top rate, until I realized that I was going to create huge amounts of timing delay. Doug Burd said, "Well, it doesn't look computer enough," and he was right of course. He said, "I think we should keep in mind that computers don't do curves. They do straight lines", but my argument then was, "Hang on a minute. If you could do enough straight lines and they're short enough, and you put them all together, you get a curve."

Computers did do wonderful curves, but we wanted a low-tech look.

The earlier stuff we did still looked a bit like Hitchhiker's as it is now, actually, except that it was more technical. It's like automotive design or aircraft design, something like that. The look and feel of it was very similar. The only thing I disagreed about was he wanted to make things much more angular.

But very often, nobody had time to criticize anyway. We were so tight with deadlines that BBC were taking 16 ml rushes straight into editing, as soon as we'd completed them and nobody had time to change anything.

Did you have to do any storyboarding?

We always did storyboards, yes. I've actually still got quite a few of them; just my rough scribbles. They would probably have been seen in production

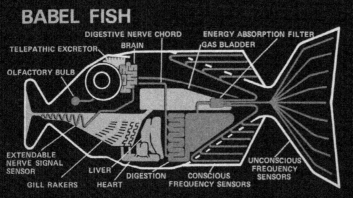

BABEL FISH

ENERGY ABSORPTION FILTER
DIGESTIVE NERVE CHORD
GAS BLADDER
BRAIN
TELEPATHIC EXCRETOR
OLFACTORY BULB

EXTENDABLE
NERVE SIGNAL
SENSOR
LIVER
DIGESTION
CONSCIOUS
FREQUENCY SENSORS
UNCONSCIOUS
FREQUENCY
SENSORS
GILL RAKERS
HEART

THE BABEL FISH IS SMALL, YELLOW, LEECHLIKE,
AND PROBABLY THE ODDEST THING IN THE UNIVERSE.
IT FEEDS ON BRAIN WAVE ENERGY, ABSORBING ALL

meetings, which I had to attend. I seem to remember they were quite frequent; there were a couple for every episode.

Nobody was asking me to contribute anything, I was just asked to be there. There were mostly discussions about set design, building, headlights, camera work, that sort of stuff, and lots of script meetings.

We had a huge amount of freedom, as a result really. I only remember one occasion having to ask for a meeting about a particular episode. It was about monetary units. There was a particular "Flainian Pobble Bead". It was worth a lot of galactic currency, shown by a long line of zeroes after the initial number. We couldn't think of a way to make it look interesting, but in the end, we turned them into cartoon faces that blew raspberries and stuck their tongues out. That came directly from Douglas. He suggested that, because we were at a loss.

Did you get a soundtrack to work from as well?

Yes. We always started with the voice-over track right at the

very beginning. Basically, all I did was mark off lengths of film where actions or places where things had to be at a certain time, then transfer all of that to my storyboard.

Were you familiar with The Hitchhiker's Guide to the Galaxy before you took the job?

I had heard a couple of episodes of the radio series literally only just before this all cropped up. I was not a long-term follower or reader by any chance. I'd never read any of the books. It was Kevin Davis, the assistant, who was the catalyst for all of this. He got us into some troubling scrapes from

time to time because he was so enthusiastic to do stuff. He got us some title sequence work for Gerry Anderson. I had a little bit of a sticky relationship with Gerry Anderson.

We'd been working on Terrahawks titles for a while. Kevin's enthusiasm got us that job, even though we had too much work on at the time. Kevin, like a lot of fans back then, had done some work for Gerry for free. When he heard about the title sequence that was up for grabs, Kevin was dying to do it but he would have to do it through us. He was literally begging us to do it. Kevin promised us that he would do it all himself if we took him off the other work duties. He promised he would run the project without any need for any other input from us – the rest of the company. Unfortunately, it didn't quite work out like that and we had to step in to help him out in the end. I ended up having to deal with Gerry Anderson, which I didn't enjoy but generally, Kevin's enthusiasms were very enjoyable and very positive.

We did get some commercials as a result of working with Gerry. We also got the Max Headroom background animations for "Max Headroom the movie" which was made as a pilot before the series came out.

The Hollywood version of Hitchhiker's was for me very disappointing.

Yes, me too. I was looking forward to seeing a whole new explosion of our approach to the graphics because to me the graphics were always such an integral part of the storytelling of the series. To actually leap from one place to another and to inject bits of humour that were not possible as part of a live script. I was so disappointed when I saw it. I wasn't expecting anything from the live-action except scenery that didn't shake and stuff like that. But I was expecting something really exciting from the graphics and I didn't find it, so I was quite disappointed. The technology is such now, that the possibilities are endless, compared with what we were dealing with originally, anyway. The tools available had almost no limitations - maybe that was the problem, I don't know.

In the TV series, Marvin (the Paranoid Android) was big and angular, and looked like a very depressed character. But in the film, they changed the design to be this really futuristic looking perky little robot. I thought that was a really bad mistake.

In the TV series, he was clunky too, and his servos gave out a hiss when he moved. The movie Marvin was too shiny and plasticky. I suppose they were aiming for something cuter really, which I feel was a big mistake, and nothing to do with the Marvin everyone was expecting.

I think that the movie lost track of the atmosphere, of the culture, the mythology, or whatever it was that the earlier material kind of generated. It tried to be too Hollywood, although I guess there must have been people that liked it.

MADNESS

Madness were the first band that I really "got into" – helped by two factors – one was that all newly acquired friends at the new school were big fans of theirs, and also it was a time when their mixture of New Wave melancholy and SKA music was sweeping all before them in the charts. Throw in some really energetic and fun pop videos and, well, who didn't love Madness? You would need a heart of stone to dislike them…

Woody Woodgate

Woody is the drummer in the band, though he has also been involved with Voice of the Beehive, and others. He was the quiet one in the band, but is a very friendly chap.

So how did the music come into your life?

Well, I grew up in west London with my brother Nick. He's 15 months younger than me. Mum and Dad were arguing and leaving the house one by one. Suddenly, Mum was not around. Then Dad was not around. We ended up living with my dad. He got custody of us. He moved to Camden Town about '64. My mum then became a weekend mom.

It was great because my brother and I lived a quiet bohemian lifestyle because my dad was working. He was a professional photographer. We were mainly brought up with nannies and au pair girls. We were quite free spirits. We did whatever we wanted. When Nick started to play the guitar, I picked up the one thing which I was good at which is drumming. Then we formed a band, as you do when you are a kid. It was pretty good. Living in Camden Town was great. We used to play with all of the kids in the estate across the road off Agar Grove.

Were you a goody-goody kid growing up?

I suppose I was intelligent enough and eloquent enough to untangle my way out of situations. I didn't go for many of my lessons at school. I don't know if that's being good or bad. I'm certainly not violent nor have I ever stolen anything obviously. I was lucky enough to not be in want for anything in the sense that my dad was well paid and we lived in a nice house in Camden.

It rubs me up a little bit when Madness is regarded as being a working-class band. Actually, the truth of it is that most of the band came from parents who worked in decent jobs, were quite well educated, artistic and went to nice schools in Hampstead and that sort of area. I mean it's because we weren't flowery in our lyrics. We talked about normal people's lives and people we'd grown up with and we observed life as it was.

When you started to play with your brother, can you remember your first gig?

It was a pub in Chalk Farm near the train station. I think they do still put on gigs there now, upstairs over the pub. I can't remember what the hell it's called. No, I do remember it had a load of old guys in there - locals. A proper "boozer" type of pub. I remember there was a queue outside. Everyone was saying "How old are these boys? They're not allowed in here." "16, 16 they're all 16.", but they let us in and it was great.

After a couple of gigs in schools, we formed a little band called "Steel Erection" which OK, is a bit of a smutty name, but when we went over to visit Mum the first part of the Westway was built around the Baker Street area, and there was a load of this scaffolding stuff. They had hundreds of signs that said, "Beware steel erection." I just thought it sounded hysterical. Thinking it was quite rude. It stuck with me. When with my brother, I'd be very childish. We were thinking of calling it chicken lips because chickens obviously don't have lips, they have beaks but anyway…

How did Madness come together?

It was all due to Steel Erection. All the people we hung out with at that time came from the Camden area. I met "Bedders" years ago (Mark Bedford). I met him before

he could even play the bass. He turned up at my mate's houses, with me and Nick and he was beginning to learn to play.

Garry Dovey was a good mate of mine. He was a drummer. They were two founder members of what later became Madness, along with Mike Barson and Chris Foreman, and Lee Thompson. I saw them play a gig, at "Willy Nilly's", under the name "The Invaders". My brother was in another band by then and they were playing at the same venue.

There were two things that struck me. First was that they were bloody awful but I really liked them. I really did. They had something about them that was just so different. It wasn't just the fact that they weren't polished musicians like everyone else, they just had something special. The other thing that really struck me is how frustrated I was with Garry Dovey, the drummer. I was thinking, "I'm better than him! I could do that.".

Soon after that, I heard that Garry had left the band. I rang Bedders, and I said, "Any chance of me getting in?" He said 'Yes, Come on down.' So, I went down and then I met these kind of threatening, unfriendly people. Mike was very brisk in particular.

I'd heard about this singer called Suggs that they had. I'd heard that he'd been sacked because he wanted to watch football instead of going to practice with the band, but he was back in the band again. He was a Chelsea fan which was good because I am. That was a positive point there. Suggs walked in flanked by two rather large skinheads. They looked awfully aggressive. I kind of wondered what the hell have I gotten myself into! But actually,

they were a really nice bunch once the atmosphere had thawed out. They just gave me the songs that they'd been performing from that gig I saw and I played those.

Mark was the most demanding. Mark knew what he wanted and he would sometimes kick me off the drum kit, sit down himself and try to play what he wanted me to play. It was interesting because I was a very flary drummer. And he would say, "No, just play it simple, play it simple." It suited the songs because a lot of them were simple rock and roll songs.

"The Prince" was one of their first records – they played it on a cassette and asked me to play along with it, but because of the loud recording, I couldn't hear what the hell the drummer was playing. I just kind of made it up. I'd never played reggae or blue

beat or Ska in my life. I didn't know what the hell it was because I'd never listened to that music. I sensed I was on probation.

We did a series of gigs in London. They picked up incredibly fast and we'd get really good crowds. We packed out The Hope and Anchor in Kensington. We did two or three nights there. The alarm bells went out to record companies so they all attended.

We thought we'd get a residency somewhere. We picked a pub that had a little stage. It was absolutely tiny. It had a few beer crates stacked together with a board over the top in a corner of a room in the back of the Dublin Castle in Camden. It was a very folky, crafty venue for individuals playing with acoustic guitars. We thought we'd go in and see if we could get a gig there. We did and of course, they

didn't have room for big crowds at the Dublin Castle. The place got jam-packed. We did that for a couple of weeks and people were spilling out into the street. We did a gig with The Specials, which got the press on board and it was a bit of a buzz. The Specials had a flock of record companies following them by then.

We decided that we needed to record a single. We had to find the money to do that and did a little set, three songs – The Prince, Madness and My girl. We recorded those at Pathway which is where Elvis Costello recorded his first album, a tiny little eight-track studio in North London. Once the single came out on under the Two-Tone Records label, other record companies all wanted to sign us. Dave Robinson, who was the head of Stiff Records, invited us to his wedding. We did a little gig, and he seemed very particularly in tune with us (pardon the pun) and so we signed for Stiff Records. Then from there, history was made! We put out an album and it did well, a few singles too – This all happened within a year of me joining the band!

The post-punk scene seemed overly serious. Do you think the world was crying out for a bit of fun in music again?

I think we needed an antidote to it didn't we really? We needed something to just cheer things up a little bit. It was hard times and the punk thing opened up other attitudes. It also opened up music to smaller bands – the DIY punk ethos opened up a lot more venues too - before that, you couldn't get gigs for a lot of money unless you had an agent. How in the world do you get an agent unless you'd done some gigs? Record companies were signing dinosaurs and all the big rock bands were really getting self-indulgent. Punk kind of swept away that and opened it up for everyone, but we brought music back in because let's face it punk was hardly tuneful for the most part! I suppose we wanted to laugh again, and the music scene found a special zone for us and didn't really analyze us too much.

The music from Prince Buster and in general, ska and blue beat and all that kind of up-tempo fast exciting, fun music hadn't been played by a young generation in the UK or Europe before. Also, the UK was becoming more ethnically diverse – and we were probably the first generation where growing up around people from different cultural backgrounds was normal. We thought nothing of it. The multicultural society that I grew up in had to be exploited at some point by the music industry and we helped them.

One thing that I used to love were the pop videos because they looked so much fun to make. They were obviously quite low-budget for the time but great to watch. How did you come up with the ideas?

I think we used to sit around and just suggest weird stuff, have a laugh and then say "let's go and see if we can do it!" We used to say, "Oh there's a canal up the road, let's all go down there and do some filming," and you just make up something funny. Everyone used to make up a funny joke and try and film it, it was a laugh really. I suppose it kind of annoyed us a bit when our band wasn't given big budgets to go to the Bahamas and go there and sail in yachts and squat around looking cool like everyone else seemed to be doing. It wasn't really us though, we'd just go down the road and have a laugh.

The Baggy Trousers video was fun. That was brilliant, Lee just thought "I want to fly" but the poor sod had no idea what we had in store for him! We all talked to Kathy Wise a professional stunt performer from the theatre. It all cost a fortune to make someone look like they were flying in a safety suit using wires. I think someone in the band must know how to hire a crane cheaply – so they did – We put a coat hanger in the back of his suit and dangled him from some old shipping wire. I don't think he suggested anything else after that…

It actually looked great in the end – the lighting bleached out the wire so you couldn't see it, but to be honest, we didn't care if they were visible – it would have been funnier if they had been.

How did the songwriting work in Madness, did you all have input?

Everyone used to come in with snippets of songs or have whole songs or Chris would whistle a tune. We could all write. We were just quite lucky to be in a band full of writers I suppose.

I wrote a solo album. In Your Mind. The reason for that was I did an album a couple of years before that with my brother Nick called the Magic Line where Nick and I played everything and Nick sang. Quite a little album really, I was very, very pleased to do it. What made me kind of go off and do my own album with another singer was simply because Nick was unable to do live gigs. We tried a few at the Dublin Castle which were quite successful but it wasn't right for Nick because Nick's a schizophrenic.

I've been trying for years to bring to the attention of the world the

fact that you're not an ax-wielding maniac if you're a schizophrenic. You can be as lovely as my brother. He happens to have this condition that restricts his day-to-day movement. He struggles to cope with the world. Apart from that, his ability to be a singer-songwriter is not diminished by that illness. Just because he's got schizophrenia doesn't mean he's stupid or he can't play his guitar or write amazing music. In this case, he was unable to go and promote and sing and get out there the music that we'd put together.

After that album, Nick and I still had another whole album's worth of stuff to play. I talked to Nick about it and I thought, "Would you mind if I got another singer in who can sing this stuff and then we can go and do some gigs?" He went, "Absolutely fine." I think Nick was actually quite relieved that he didn't have the pressure of singing on it. I put it out under my name. In all reality, it was a joint effort from my brother and I. It was just under the guise of Woody Woodgate. Credit must be given to my brother who is an incredibly talented songwriter and musician.

The style of Madness songs changed over time becoming more reflective – why was that?

Yes. I think when you're on the road all year round, you lose touch with reality a bit. Your only interaction with life is what you see on the news and what's around in the media at the time. We began to write more – we were reflecting on the world around us as opposed to our experiences in day-to-day life because our experiences in day-to-day life, unfortunately, narrowed down to getting on a tour bus, going up a motorway, doing a gig, and then staying in a hotel. Then, the next thing you do, you're stuck in a studio writing

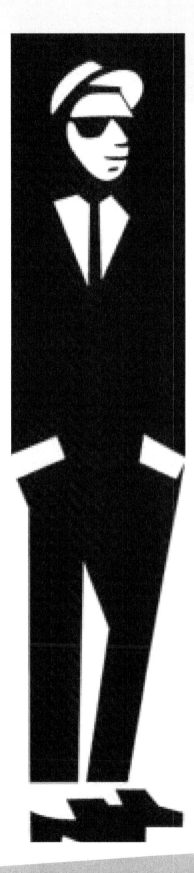

new songs and performing them live and the cycle goes around.

That actually prompted Mike to leave the band in '83 I think it was, '82, '83, where he saw it as being a never-ending cycle. He couldn't do it anymore. In a sense, the band, on reflection, look back at that time and think, "You know what? He was right. All we needed was a break." We needed a break and to go and live in the normal world for a while so we could start writing about our experiences with people and life. It does get a bit sour when you start getting all serious and reflecting on life. Then, that was part of our journey, our path.

You went on to play in Voice of the Beehive as well, didn't you?

Yes. I loved it. It was brilliant because I went straight out of Madness. It was like being chucked in the deep end of a swimming pool. I went, "Oh my God. I'm 26 years old, 25, 26 years old and my life's over. What do I do now?" Then, along came this offer to play with Voice of the Beehive. It was just right up my street because it was guitar-based pop and rock. Very catchy, but with a bit of bite, good guitars. Mike's a great guitarist, Mike Jones that is. I tell you what. It was seven years, some of the best years of my life really because I toured the world with a great band and had a flipping blast really because I'm very fond of them.

The music industry has changed a lot, hasn't it since those days? You don't seem to hear great albums anymore. What do you think about that?

Well, I just think that you and I think what you just said is exactly along the lines of how I

feel as well. I like an album. It's definitely an art form. That is the way it's gone. It's like anything, you fine tune things as you go along. Car manufacturing, they've sorted everything out from the windscreen wipers right down to the aerodynamic shape of a car. They're refining it to such a point that every single car looks the same. It's the same with the music industry. It doesn't matter because there will always be great music out there. I really believe that. If you feed them this generic crap long enough, people just get sick of it.

It might change. Punk came along to shake everything up, and I think in the music industry, there will always be people who come along and shake everything up. I'm an eternal optimist, really. I don't really care about The X Factor and all that stuff, because it's just not in my world. My world is surrounded by musicians I love, and I'm doing music I like. I only know people that think like you do, and I do. That's the people I'm going to surround myself with. I don't really care. I don't care how people buy their music. I don't care if a large majority of people are brainwashed by crap, because I know that actually, there's an undercurrent of people who are accessing the most amazing music.

Top of The Pops was different. You had so much diversity in music, and that programme tried its best to show it because it was the only way to get it out to people. And people bought it. You would see punk bands, heavy rock, heavy metal, and pop all in the one show. But that is all in the past. I just hope that people "got us" as a band. That we made a lot of people happy. And still do. That's all that matters in the end.

Fighting Fantasy Books

People of my age group that were a bit geeky had all dabbled in role-playing to some extent, but it was difficult to organise a place to do it, and to get a bunch of 13 and 14 year olds to meet up at weekends was nigh-on impossible. I had managed to get hold of a copy of Dungeons and Dragons, and set myself up as a "Dungeon Master", but even bribing my friends with sweets didn't work after the second week. Then suddenly "Fighting Fantasy" books were a big thing at our school– the cooler geekier kids (usually the ones that were middle class and had more cash), began to appear with a book and dice at lunchtimes. We were intrigued – The books were just about cheap enough for me to afford too - £1.50 in 1982.

AND I could play the game on my own – Ideal! They were a huge success, and lots and lots of books appeared in the series – brilliant stories along with great artwork too!

Ian Livingstone

Ian Livingstone was one of the guys (along with Steve Jackson) to bring Role-Playing games to the mass market in the UK. Not only did he found Games Workshop, but he also founded White Dwarf magazine, and then went on to write a good number of Fighting Fantasy books, before going off to make computer games with Eidos. He is back writing a new series of Fighting Fantasy books…

You were instrumental in bringing role-playing in general to the masses with Games Workshop. Tell us about that. You were the first person to bring over the Dungeons and Dragons games for sale?

That's right. I was sharing a flat in Shepherd's Bush with two old school friends: Steve Jackson and John Peake. We used to play board games as a hobby and we decided to try and turn our hobby into some sort of business. We started a newsletter which we sent out to everybody we knew and one of the copies ended up on the desk of Gary Gygax in Lake Geneva, Wisconsin. Although we hadn't sent it to him directly, he read it and wrote back to us saying that "I love your newsletter! Here's this game I've just invented called "Dungeons and Dragons."" This is back right at the beginning of 1975 and we played it, became immediately obsessed with it and wrote back to him to order 6 copies. On the back of that order, we got an exclusive distribution agreement for the whole of Europe so we became the official distributors of D&D in Europe. The company we started was called Games Workshop and over time we moved out of our flat. We went to the States and signed up all the other young games companies, and then started expanding the company. By then we had started opening our own

retail shops in 1978 and that's how D&D got started in the UK. We started a magazine called "Owl and the Weasel" which was an instant print fanzine. Then we realised that we needed to get a bit more professional so we decided that we should create a new glossy magazine and we called it " White Dwarf". This covered the whole hobby not just Dungeons and Dragons. All games at that time got featured in "White Dwarf" and it became the centre for the hobby people. They subscribed to it, wrote about it and wrote for it too. It was a bold move to put out a brand new glossy magazine but it certainly paid off – it's nice to see it still going so successfully these days.

How did you manage to get it into all of the other shops? Were retailers a bit worried about it being a minority hobby?

It just took time in the early days of "Workshop" . It was very, very difficult to get the company off the ground. We didn't have any money so we had to live in a van for three months. All our money went into stock . We moved our business from our flat to a small office which was quite a big risk so we couldn't afford anywhere else to live for 3 months. We were living the dream so it didn't matter.

I was pretty obsessed with the Fighting Fantasy books when I was much younger. Were you aware of the other 'choose-your-own-adventure' books that were out at the time?

No, "Warlock of Firetop Mountain", the first book, came out in 1982 in the "Fighting Fantasy" range and that had the first branching narrative with a game system attached to it. There were other interactive books at the time which had the 'choose-your-own-adventure' series. Then they had 'choose-your-own-chapter' .So we wanted to have an experience that was similar to a role playing game so that's why we added the combat system.

Is that how the dream came about to be able to play a role playing game on your own?

Yes, we substituted the Games Master or the Dungeon Master with a book and turned it into a multiple choice. It was a pretty original idea at the time and , although there were many ways of going through the book, there was only one correct way. We were hugely successful in the 1980s with "Warlock of Firetop Mountain", "The Forest of Doom","City of Thieves" and "Deathtrap Dungeon". Those were brilliant times and now they've just been republished by Scholastic which is great.

How did you pitch the idea to Puffin? Did you write the book first then try to pitch the idea?

No, we used to run these things called Games Day. We used to have these events in a hall in London. We had other companies with stands at the shows at Games Day and one of them was Penguin Books. The editor Geraldine Cook was bemused by the idea of everyone playing D&D in the hall and she asked Steve and I if we'd write a book about this hobby of role playing games. We suggested that,rather than writing a book about the hobby, we could write a book that gives you the experience of playing the role playing game. She thought that was a great idea so Steve and I set about creating the game system by creating the branching narrative of a game system. We called it "Magic Quest" and over time "Magic Quest" evolved into the "Warlock of Firetop Mountain" which Penguin books published in August of 1982.

How does the creative process work when you design a book? Do you plan it out on a map first or is it a flow chart. How exactly do you go about it?

I have the idea for the plot and then start structuring a flow chart from the ground up. Nothing on the flow chart is predetermined; it all happens on the fly. So it's very much old school design but it certainly works for me. I then go back and through it because you have multiple branching paths so you have to make sure it's not too hard, not too easy, and make the economy work. You have to make sure there aren't any loops and that there is a satisfying way of going through it that challenges the reader and excites at the same time. There are many layers to that and it's not as easy as it sounds.

I loved how some of the books had other characters that you could join forces with some times and sometimes you were either helped or betrayed. Were you ever tempted to be really evil and have lots of sudden death situations involving the non-player characters? Were you tempted to make it a little bit too hard?

I think it is nice just to give the reader someone to go adventuring with. In "Death Trap Dungeon", you defended the barbarian non-player character if you wanted to, whilst knowing at the same time that only one of you would be able to get through alive. So then it came down to having to fight him to the death at the end of the book which I understand a lot of readers got upset about. I like to have a bit of interaction with non-player characters because I think it adds a richness to the experience rather than just doing it all by yourself.

Were there any books that you had to alter dramatically for whatever reason?

No, they were all pretty much accepted straight away which was great. They needed editing, of course, to balance it, but storylines were never changed

Who was in charge of organising the artwork for the books?

Initially we did. We convinced Puffin that we should use our Games Workshop artists and give it a real, very exciting, dramatic art so "Warlock of Firetop Mountain" had Russ Nicholson doing the interiors. Peter Andrew Jones did the cover and then I started working with Ian McCaig, who did all the covers for "City of Thieves", "Forest of Doom", "Deathtrap Dungeon", and the internals as well on two of those books. He went on to be an incredible artist who went on to create Darth Maul for George Lucas and Star Wars

So tell me about the new books?

There has been a resurgence in "Fighting Fantasy". Those people who read them in the 1980s have now got their own kids and they are telling them that they should read these books. Normally children reject out of hand anything their parents say but I am delighted to say today's kids seem to like "Fighting Fantasy" because it resonates with their video games mentality and their way of reading and working. It's been a very pleasant revival. Scholastic are the largest publisher of children's books in the world and have the rights for the UK . It was the 35th anniversary last year so I wrote a new one for the relaunch of the

Do you think you'll ever retire?

No, no chance. I love the hobby too much to want to think about retiring.

I've seen some computer versions of the "Fighting Fantasy" books. Are you planning to turn more books into games?

There's every possibility that might happen. Tin Man did a great job of making apps out of many of our books and also they did a really nice version of "Warlock of Firetop Mountain" on STEAM and it's now available on mobile. It still shows the texts and the pictures as if it was from the book but the character moves through a 3D dungeon. The dungeon follows as you explore the world so it's a nice hybrid between the video games and the books. More recently Nomad games have developed "Fighting Fantasies Legends" and have just released their "Deathtrap Dungeon Portal Trilogy" . That's a lovely game which is a card based RPG where you power your dice. It's got rogue elements to it as well so it's a top down veiw of the world as you explore it. They did an amazing job.

series.
It's called "The Port of Peril"; four came out recently; there were six before so we carried on. It's great to see that they are still relevant after all these years. 35 years on and "Fighting Fantasy" is alive and well.

What did you think of the other books that followed your books such as the "Lone Wolf" books?

I've never read one to be honest. It's flattering that people wanted to copy the format and put out their own editions but I've never read one. A lot of the people who wrote these books used to work for us. Joe Dever and Gary Chalk used to work for us at Games Workshop and left to do their own, to do "Lone Wolf".

What do you think are the differences between yourselves and Steve's books?

I don't read other people's books. I like to try and maintain my own style without being influenced by anybody else's game books so I read science fiction books, comics and look at art work. Some say however that these books are usually more difficult than mine and the author likes to jump around genres. For example, one was Science Fiction, the next horror and then he even did superheroes too! I set most of my books in Alliansia and it was more of a coherent world. It had some abilities different to other worlds that we enjoyed so there was a connection between my books.

THE VAPORS

TURNING JAPANESE

David Fenton

I first heard The Vapors in one of my late-night scans through the radio stations under the covers of my bed when I should have been asleep. I'd already discovered pop music, but my ears were searching for something a little different. And there they were on a local radio station playing "Turning Japanese" which became the single they were better known for. Although the single hit the charts, their music differed to most other groups I was listening to in that they had a much more sophisticated song structure – and also, I was still at the age where even implied naughty words were hilarious. Apparently "turning Japanese was the face you made when you were ahem "self-pleasuring".

David Fenton was the founding member of The Vapors, and was responsible for writing the majority of their songs. He has also produced music for many other bands, and The Vapors are back touring again after a few years apart.

What were your early years like?

I had a younger brother, and we got on fine together. I also had an elder brother who looked after us a bit. My dad was a headmaster though, so that made it a bit tougher. You had to be good in school, all that sort of stuff. I'd say I had a happy childhood; my parents were great. It was entirely different then. I grew up in the '50's and even having a car was seen as something of a luxury. Even TV sets were rare. Most people I knew had a radio, and a record player. TVs came along much later in our neighbourhood, and I wouldn't say I'm that old.

I used to go to bed with a small radio and listen to the pirate stations at night. Whatever was playing, I liked the English groups such as The Kinks, The Who, Small Faces, particularly. The Beatles, Rolling Stones - the usual crop. I had friends that were also interested in music, and they used to buy different albums. We used to be interested in what was going on on the west coast of America particularly.

What was the eureka moment when you decided you wanted to learn how to play an instrument and become a musician?

It was watching Top of the Pops thinking I can do that. I want to do that. I was about 10, and I was on holiday down in Bournemouth with my parents and myself and my younger brother were given the offer of being taken to a funfair along the High Street where the Beatles were playing. That really clinched it for me. All those screaming girls and everything. That was 1963. The girls screaming were louder than the amplifiers on stage. They just didn't have sound systems like we have now. The band were getting drowned out. I got my first guitar when I was about 10. A second-hand acoustic model. I started making up chords and working out how to tune it and play. I remember learning what chords were and basically self-taught from that, using chord books. As I got older, I improved, until I was good enough to feel confident enough to see if I could make it on stage, though I was still a school boy. Because at the time I couldn't afford a car, and I couldn't afford an electric amp. I was playing in local folk clubs, acoustically, by myself, although I did have a little band with two acoustic guitars and a bloke on Bongos for a while. We called that band "Magician". I continued playing in folk clubs. I was quite influenced by people such as Roy Harper and the acoustic guitarists, simply because I could only afford to play locally.

The Vapors really was my first proper rock band. By which time I'd taken a job and saved up some money. This would be in the mid- 1970s probably. We started playing a few gigs, but the drummer and bass player were quite young, 18 and straight out of school – they had just completed their A levels and their parents persuaded them to go on and do their degrees, rather than go full-time with the band. So that line-up that I had put together soon fell apart and I was looking around Guildford for replacements. A couple of other local bands had fortuitously split-up around the same time, and some of these band members joined The Vapors.

How does the song writing work in The Vapors?

I tend to write the songs. Everyone can have their input but if something doesn't sound right to me, then I ask them to change it. me, then I ask them to change it. It's as democratic as it can be, but someone's got to have overall charge to settle any disputes if there are two people with different opinions. But I usually come up with the song ideas in the first place and the way I played the songs will also affect how the rest of the band play their parts of the song. I have to keep that in mind when I write.

The Vapors had their first break when Bruce Foxton of the Jam spotted you?

Yes, he just happened to be in a pub we were playing in. It was at The White Lion near Guildford. Must have been about 20 people there all together that night, including the people at the bar. Our bass player Steve, had recognised Bruce and approached him after the gig. Bruce said he loved it and had a great time. He liked the band; he liked the gig and did we want to do a couple of nights on The Jam tour. That was May '79, June '79. Which we obviously agreed to do. And it was during those two nights that John Weller (Paul Weller's father) saw us. John was managing The Jam, and both he and Bruce approached us to ask if they could manage us. That's how it started out, from a chance meeting in a pub just outside Guildford to getting gigs with The Jam and being offered professional management.

And that led to offers of record deals, both from Polydor, (which was the label The Jam were on) and also United Artists, which is the label we eventually signed to. That was a really fortunate night because a lot of things came out of that.

Did Bruce change your sound?

No, not at all. He'd make comments on whether he liked it

or not, but no, he didn't make us change anything, nor did John. They were happy for us to carry on as we were. We were very proficient musically, and had tight sets. We sounded different to a lot of the bands coming through at the time too. There was a lot of seriousness. Even Mods were turning political. I mean, don't get me wrong, we had our moments, and had a serious side, but our music was fun, and I think people needed something that they could forget their problems to.

What was it like touring with The Jam?

It was great fun. Like I said, we'd been playing pubs with 20 people in. Doing "2000 seaters" was amazing. It's scary but we held our own. It was impressive doing gigs of that size but we ended up doing bigger venues, and then we went to Australia too not long afterwards. It was all good fun and it was all useful experience.

What was it like when "Turning Japanese" became such a big hit and you were suddenly thrust into the limelight on "Top of the Pops"?

It was amazing. I couldn't believe it. From writing the song in my flat in Guildford to hearing it in my flat in Guildford on the radio, just made the whole world seem a lot smaller. It's a fantastic feeling. And I was surprised at how quickly the song caught on. Everything seemed to happen very quickly.

What was filming like on Top of the Pops?

It was difficult. Mainly because you're miming. You're supposed to re-record a new version of it in the BBC studio beforehand, due to union rules, but few people ever

did. You're just miming along to your own record.

The funny thing was they did two or three takes of the song, because they weren't happy with the camera angles or whatever. They'd constantly move the audience around, and the cameras. One of the shots they left in was when Howard dropped his drumsticks and walked around the drums to pick them up and the drums are still playing. Why didn't they use a different clip for that part of the song, because they did three or four run-throughs? I was amazed!

Was "Turning Japanese" actually about "w*nking"?

No, it wasn't. It's just a love song. It wasn't until we got to America that the yanks thought it was an English phrase meaning masturbating. It wasn't an English phrase meaning masturbating, but if anything, the Americans almost made it an English phrase about that and quite liked the joke and the facial contortions that go with it. Just to make the interviews a bit more interesting we used to say, "Yes, it is," and then "no it's not." Just to keep the joke going and only telling the truth half the time. You see, it can get very boring doing interview-after-interview. You do sessions of interviews for the record company and they'd be asking the same questions over-and-over-and-over again. It got exhausting, so we just made it a bit more fun.

The sound of The Vapors evolved slowly over time – did your song writing techniques change?

I'm not sure about that, yes, I write different songs but then I like writing

all sorts of different songs. Reggae, rock, you name it. The difference between the first album and the second album was a different producer, I think. They kept pushing for a really clean AM radio sound. Dave Tickle, who was producer on the second album, went for a more raucous sound because that's what we asked for, that's what we wanted. Something a bit more rock and roll than the very clean records that the previous producer had created on the first album. I'm happy with both albums because the records are still playing on the radio, they still stand up, and they still sound good.

What was the record company (United Artists) like to work with?

Mixed views. Firstly, within about six months of us signing, EMI bought out United Artists and we got inherited by an enormous conglomerate what seemed like joining the civil service compared to our previous label. United Artists was a great little company with about a dozen acts on it. There were The Buzzcocks, The Stranglers, The Gang of Four, Dr Feelgood…etc. and you could walk in any door in the building whenever you wanted to speak to any department.

An "open door" policy - you could even go and talk to the Managing Director without an appointment. It was very friendly. Great people and if they liked what we were doing, we liked the way they worked. Then to get inherited by EMI and the staff there were mostly made redundant. Suddenly, we didn't know anyone. Nobody there had even signed us up, they'd inherited us. They didn't much like us, they were far too busy with Duran Duran and Kate Bush and all these other artists which they seemed to deem much more important than us.

It went from absolutely brilliant to absolutely terrible. The follow up single was "News at Ten" which was number three in the charts, when the problems began. We had problems contacting our manager John. Obviously, he was helping "The Jam" as well as ourselves, but they were number one in the charts, and were touring, and often on the other side of the world to us, and it was the days before mobile phones. It was difficult to track both them and John down. We often found John was in France when we were in New York, or the other way around. It was just awkward. Everything began to fall apart. As I said, despite our chart success, we had no fans in the record company, as it were.

The real last straw was going in to a meeting with the A&R head who came down to the studio where we were rehearsing after the tour, to listen to what would have been by then our seventh single. He said, "Yes, fine." And took us all for a drink and a sandwich afterwards, patting us on the back - and then he went back to the office and

cancelled the actual recording session without telling us. Why couldn't he have told us to our faces? That was really the final straw and I left the band and that was the end of it. I just felt I was fighting everything uphill. We'd lost our record company, we'd lost our manager, there was no one there to help us really.

What did you do after the Vapors?

Live sound engineering, managing bands, and I did a bit of recording production. I have been in various other bands myself that I didn't front, but wrote for. I've kept on going, and it's been fun.

Do you enjoy sound engineering more than being in a band?

I prefer being in a band, I don't have all those worries that a sound engineer has, I just do my bit. I know it won't sound too bad because the amp's all set up the way I want it. There shouldn't be too many things to correct for the sound engineer. It's a nervous experience being a sound engineer, getting the best sound you can for a band when you may not have heard them before. It's always tricky. By the same token being in a band and not having worked with a sound engineer before - well - they're both a bit nerve-wracking.

The Vapors had 35 years off from each other and then got back together again in 2016. We did try once before in about 2001, but it was really difficult to organize rehearsals because people had job commitments. Ed was working for the BBC. He was quite often abroad doing holiday programs, and this caused us problems, but we were understanding, as people

have to earn a living. This time round with the band though, I've retired, so that I can do "anytime, anywhere". That sits a bit better for everyone else!

What do you think of the way that the music industry has evolved with digital downloads?

I prefer the old way, frankly. Back then, it was 50p to get into a gig and the album costs five quid or thereabouts. Now it's the complete reverse, it's 40 or 50 quid to go and see the band who now more or less give the actual singles and albums away for nothing. I think that's wrong. Anyway, we can't help that. That's the way it is now. That's the way it works these days.

I think X Factor and programs like that have done a disservice to the music industry, really, because everyone thinks that firstly karaoke's all right, (which it isn't). And secondly that the only sort of music that should exist is the sort of stuff that would be on X Factor. Which is bland Pop music. They've just limited everything now. Everyone thinks that that's the only thing that's going to get anywhere. Any other type of singer or band is invalid, which obviously is wrong. I don't think Simon Cowell has done much to help the music industry. He's made himself a lot of money and a few artists a bit of money. But as an industry he's not helped it one bit. Terrible contracts though. Even the ones that win, don't have a guaranteed career. But The Vapors made our mark during a relative golden age in music, and I have to be happy with that.

DUNE

Dune is an epic series of books (Written by the late Frank Herbert) that has a unique mixture of Science Fiction, Spiritualism, and an almost unparalleled ambition in depth– it features a universe full of competing factions, with a story that spanned millennia. Paul Atreides is the beleaguered child of the duke, who escapes into the hostile desert of the sand planet of Dune after his father is killed in an attack by the archenemy, Baron Harkonnen. The politics are too complicated to explain in a few sentences, but the books made a big impression upon me, and I have reread them several times over.

Jim Burns

Jim Burns is an illustrator who has remained one of the top names in cover designs since the 1970s. He is known for many excellent paintings but it was his atmospheric covers on the books of the Dune series that drew me to them.

What were your impressions of the Dune books prior to working on the covers for Heretics of Dune and Eye? (part of the Dune universe)

Well I was in my late teens when the Dune books first appeared and I was an avid Science Fiction reader. I'd not really had any

preconceptions about the books – I remember finding them on a shelf, and just deciding to read them. I was already familiar with the work of the then illustrator, John Schoenherr – for me he was the definitive Dune illustrator.

I almost got to work on the film version of Dune – back when Ridley Scott was going to make it. Ridley had just finished working on Alien. He'd seen a figure in one of my Harry Harrison internal spreads for "Planet Story" that was a dead ringer for how he had envisaged Baron Harkonnen and he decided to get me on-board. I chatted to him a few times, but

the project fell through (though it was later filmed by David Lynch), and we went on to work on Blade Runner instead.

Did growing up in rural Wales inspire you to become an artist?

Well, I was born in Cardiff back in 1948. Not quite working class, but just hovering on the edge of lower and middle class, I suppose. Inspiring lower middle class, something like that?

I Grew up in South Wales. Always drawing. Drawing and reading. Head in a book. Even at a very young age. Anything fantasy based is really what I liked and so I've always been drawn to that subject matter with the kind of stuff that I paint.

We moved out of the City of Cardiff, out into the countryside when I was seven. A lot of nature around obviously! I was drawing insects and stuff like that. I could have easily become a natural history artist actually.

My school was Bassaleg Grammar… just outside Newport. My primary ambition wasn't really to be an artist then. What I really wanted to be was a pilot in the RAF.

You know the Eagle comic in the '50s? I grew up with that comic. I loved Dan Dare and I thought, If I wanted to eventually become an astronaut and to go into space, like Dan Dare, where do I start? How do you become a space pilot?

So, I applied to join the RAF back when I was 16. Went along at 17 to do the aircrew selection tests in RAF Biggin Hill and got accepted. I started training as an RAF Pilot back in 1966 when I was 18. I soloed on the Chipmunks and then on Jet Provost—I did fly solo on both types of plane. But I wasn't a very good pilot to be honest. In fact, I was bloody dangerous!

I got taken off flying, much to my huge disappointment and that of my father, who was so proud that his son was going to be a pilot. I could've stayed in the RAF doing something else, but if I couldn't fly planes then there wasn't a lot of point as far as I was concerned. I didn't want to be a Catering Officer or anything like that.

Back then you could do a Voluntary Suspension if you are still under training so I voluntarily suspended myself and came out of the RAF.

I was approaching 20 years of age. I needed to join an art college. I realized I had to take along some work to show people. I thought, "Blimey, I haven't got much." I went along to my old school where my art teacher had thankfully kept a lot of my stuff back in a big drawer. She'd hung on to some of my old school work fortunately and returned it to me as well as helping me to go through the initial application stages to get to art school.

I managed to churn out new stuff too, quite quickly and went along to Newport Art College. I was interviewed and showed my work and I managed to get in.

I spent the first year there, and then applied to go to St. Martins in London which was the best college for illustration at the time. A lot of good people came out of St Martins. I applied and managed to get in, much to my surprise.

A lot of the tutors at Art College saw the work I was doing and didn't really know what to do with me though. They didn't get this "Science Fiction" stuff at all and thought I was wasting my time.

At the Diploma Show which marked the end of the 3-year course, each of us put our art shows up. An agent came and looked at everyone's work. He spoke to me and said he thought he could find me some work. It was 1972 and at that time there was a rise in popularity in Science Fiction and book jacket illustration was big business. People such as Chris Foss and Roger Dean were big names in this industry, so I was quite excited.

When I got my results, I only actually got a lower-second which isn't a very good pass, but I had found an agent. So, I was off to a good start!

Whilst I was at St Martins, I met my future wife, Sue. She was studying in the Fine Art Department. We got together. Got married the following year, '73.

I had a great time at college. I'd call it a three-year party, basically. I can't in all honesty, say I received a lot of encouragement from the tutors - the art world around this time was probably just beginning to change in terms of their disinclination to teach anything academic and traditional. I was in the graphics and illustration department, but right through the college we had the beginnings of the fad for "conceptual work" and "de-skilling".

I think the tutors themselves were not equipped to give us much in the way of academic technical advice. I just learnt it as I went along and developed my own peculiar ways of doing things. The consequence of that it means my stuff perhaps has a particular look that people can identify as "mine", but it's probably because its technically all over the shop, and certainly not a traditional technique.

I don't want to slag St Martin's off - it was a useful experience. You're surrounded by talented people and people rub off against each other in terms of picking up ideas. It gets you into thinking the right way about illustration and art.

I was starting to get regular work by then, though It was still sort of a poor existence - they were very low paid jobs. A lot of what I was doing back then was Historical Romance, that kind of stuff. The agents usually gave us Rookies the work that no one else wanted to do. I was very thankful for that kind of work though, because it gave me a chance to begin learning how to tackle figure work.

But I built a portfolio up and eventually started to get some Science Fiction work coming in. I bought myself an airbrush round about then in 1974, and got stuck in.

I built a career and reasonably decent income and lifestyle out of painting pictures for book jackets. I was lucky to be part of that, because it gave me a couple of decades of good continuous work, both here and in the US working through my agent.

I spend a lot of time trying to get that right, I'm obsessional about detail and conviction - I like things to have conviction, that it might just exist or could be built and actually work.

I'm painting a mermaid at the moment - it's not quite an alien, but it's in the alien concept. When I decided to have a crack at her first of all, I had to find a mermaid that existed in mythology. It has to have a point of origin to me, so I did some research.

First of all, they can be strange and mysterious, and of course alluring creatures and bad luck to sailors. I found one called Thessalonike who is the mermaid of the Aegean, she is a Greek mermaid. Thessaloniki is named after her. She was the sister of Alexander the Great. She used to get very upset when he went off to wars for months, even years. She missed him so much and he was away so long that in the end she couldn't bear it and tried to commit suicide by leaping into the sea, but

When you design crafts/ space ships – mechanical things - do you think your background in the air force helped you? Your craft always look as though they have a genuine use.

That comes out of the childhood obsession with The Eagle comic, with Frank Hampson and Frank Bellamy's artwork. I think their stuff always had that organic look of '50s machinery. Other artists drew these massive space hulks that were never designed to look like they could actually fly –they were just thrown together rather than have any real formal grace to them.

Whenever I create a vessel of some sort, space craft or a car, I want it to look as though, that there is a blueprint for it somewhere, even if it's a bunch of alien blueprints, that there is a rationale to the way it looks. Machinery for me, aircraft and cars and stuff like that, I don't know the first thing about what goes on under the bonnets of the car or the jets of an airplane

really, but the primary drive is to make them look not only dramatic, but conceivable in terms of a real functional design process, either human or alien.

I want creatures and aliens to look as though there is some kind of evolution that went on there. That there is a logic to their structure.

instead of dying she turned into a mermaid. She would always ask the question of any passing sailor, "Where is Alexander?" and if they say, "Alexander is not coming back," or that he's dead, then that was doom for those sailors, and the ship would go down - she would cause its destruction. If they'd say, "He would be home soon," she would be happy and she would let them pass on...

It's not just a beautiful woman with a fishtail, it's the business of making her look like she's become something that is neither woman nor a fish. And potentially dangerous.

How did you adapt when computer-based art started to emerge?

Well, the digital art came in, in the mid to late '90s and with book publishers, the bottom line is always what counts. Why pay artists like myself quite a lot of money, because they did pay well for something that took a month to paint, when they can pay someone a hell of a lot less to turn out something very quickly in Photoshop? Someone young, fresh out of art college. A lot of us were having to look at what do were to do with the rest of our lives in terms of a career structure.

That meant not just for me, but for others too – it meant a distinct drop in income for a kick off, so we all had to make some pretty hard decisions as a family. Some people just dropped out of the illustration scene all-together or taught art or whatever. But I

persisted, I learnt how to use the computer.

I have used Photoshop myself in my digital work, I've always tried to emulate my painting style on the computer. Trying to get things out as quickly as I can, as I said, because they don't pay a lot for this sort of work.

If I was a younger man and if I'd been a 20-year-old back in the '90s and I was going to follow a life of illustration, I think I would have been very drawn to digital work. I do find it fun, and it's a nice break from the stink of the paint and turps and the physically tiring aspect of painting a larger canvas.

Sitting in front of the computer, you can almost go into automatic mode. You've got to focus obviously and want to do your best for the client, but it's a different kind of sensibility required for it to.

Some digital art I've seen is brilliant. I think there are some amazing images out there, but one thing I would say is that a lot of it does look very generic. It gets a little bit hard to differentiate between one artist and another. Good as they are. There is a digital look and slickness to a lot of it. That some say is quite soulless. I don't know about that, but there is something missing somewhere.

There are people out there for whom the computer is the devil's tool. If it doesn't involve getting messy with pigment and turps... then it's not really art.

Then there are other people who switched across-- like my good friend Fred Gambino for instance. Who switched across from being a painter to a purely digital artist and for him, that's meant his career took an upturn. He's now involved in a lot of film work.

Some are able to adopt digital tools, as a tool in the armoury, if you like, you've got it there in your studio, it's part of the way you work. That's how I like it. It's there and I feel a bit naked without my computer to be honest.

I'm also belatedly learning traditional art techniques too. I'm trying to force myself into adopting some old renaissance techniques by working on canvas

93

with oils and going about it in a rather structured and traditional way which has got centuries of people's experience behind it. You build up the painting with all the onal values and the detailed work s done in that stage. You get it all out onto the canvas without trying o mix paint - It's quite quick. Then you use transparent glazes over the top to get the depth of colour. t's a beautiful way to work.

What you do definitely, as you get older, because you've built up some experience of the world of art, if you'd like, the world of music, by being a part of it, you do start to appreciate more what went before and start to dig into it a little bit and find the true value that lies n tradition. That's not hard with art have to say, look around you and what passes for contemporary art, I can't say it amuses me very much. I find most of it absolutely tedious in the extreme.

The reason I'm doing this new style of painting - besides improving my technique - is the same reason you will find a lot of people of my vintage, who used to be book jacket artists, particularly in the US… Something happened over here, some 10 years ago. A guy named Pat Wilshire and his wife Jeannie Wilshire (who are great art collectors), discovered there's a whole bunch of artists out there who have been cut adrift, lost their way, and who were struggling to make a living.

They set up a thing called the Symposium for Imaginative Realism, Illuxcon – The Symposium of Imaginative Realism, that happens every year. All the big-name artists from the "golden era" – people such as Michael Whelan, Donato Giancola, Chris Moore, Bob Eggleton, Julie Bell, Boris Vallejo, and many others all go. We take

all of the traditionally made paintings we've been working on, plus signed prints of the older stuff. It is a collector's market for buying existing artwork or to order private commissions. That's opening a whole new bunch of possibilities for everyone. The art collectors come in, hopefully with their packed wallets and everyone is competing with each other for the contents of those wallets.

You've had a long and distinguished career in the world of Art. Were your family disappointed in you for leaving the air force, and then becoming an artist?

Yes. My Dad took on a pub, which was the worst decision he ever made. And that happened to coincide with me leaving the air force.

When I said I was going to art college, students were then seen as long haired "lay-abouts", basically. I had just started to grow my hair really long too and the really clean-cut boy that he knew had turned into this slouching art student - he was not at all happy.

Now that remained the case for a while. Then I met Sue, my wife and took her home, whilst I was still at St Martin's, and she was a great salvation for me, because she was a lovely girl and Dad thought, "Hello. God, he's done something right at long last."

But career wise, at some point, because I was making a decent enough living and we had some lovely kids and he could see that life had turned out okay for me - I'd become a well-known illustrator, he said, "Well, in the end Jim, I can see you did the right thing".

HEAVEN 17

Synthpop had been around for a while of course, and everyone seemed to like the sound – OMD, China Crisis, Depeche Mode and of course The Human League – but a darker sound was being developed, in some cases by the people behind the embryonic earlier sounds. The simplistic early Electronica music was giving way to a harder edged style, which had a darker, more angst-ridden sound. Heaven 17, who had emerged from The Human League, was pioneering the style that would eventually lead to bands such as Gary Numan, Nine Inch Nails and the Industrial Rock genre.

Martyn Ware

Martyn Ware was the keyboard genius behind many hits in the 1980s, originally with The Human League, and then with Heaven 17, as well as providing production for some of the world's biggest artists. He is now teaching a new generation of musicians.

Sheffield briefly became the focal point of exciting new bands in the 1980s. Was it grim up north?

Yes. We lived in Upperthorpe. Just off Weston Street, down from where the Arts Tower is now. Until I was about 8, we lived in a really old-fashioned Council house. Two-up two-down. Outside toilet. Three other siblings living there until I was a bit older. It was "proper poor". My dad worked for a steelworks company and my mum was a full-time mother. Then we moved to another Council house, in Burngreave, which compared to where we were living was absolute luxury. Central heating, indoor toilet. Stayed there a few years, and then we ended up in Broomhall Flats in Sheffield, which is where I spent most of my teenage years.

What sort of music were you enjoying during your adolescence?

We didn't have very much in the house, to be honest. We did have a record player though because one sister is 20 years older than me and my other sister is 10 years older than me. Their big thing was pop music, just 60s pop really, and a bit of Motown. I grew up with all of that, which was our main form of entertainment when I was growing up.

Was there any musical side to the family at all? Did you make your own music as a family?

No. There were rumours that my mum used to play piano before I was born and we used to have a piano in the house. My dad exhibited no musical talent really, but everybody seemed to love music in our family.

One of my most treasured memories of growing up is (when I was old enough) buying records and stacking them up on the auto-changer on the record player.

I would also be listening to the transistor radio at night under the sheets when I was meant to be asleep, and this led me away from the early pop that my sisters were listening to, to new types of music, and different types of songs.

Radio Luxembourg was a major part of my musical development - listening to groups like the Beach Boys. Lots of interesting American west coast bands. Lots of stuff that never got played on British radio.

I eventually started going to secondary school when I became a bit older - I went to "King Ted's" in Sheffield, and started mixing with people and developing my own musical taste. It was a very interesting time in my life.

The first record I ever purchased was Deep Purple in Rock. The main blossoming of my love of music though, I suppose, was the emergence of "Prog Rock". I'm a big fan of King Crimson, Emmerson Lake and Palmer, Van de Graaf Generator etc. But I've always kept my love of pop music.

I've always had incredibly eclectic tastes. I think that's a major influence on the kind of stuff that I, historically, have created.

How did the emergence of Electronica bands such as Kraftwerk influence you?

That was my second musical phase, really. I was always interested in anything that had any kind of electronic basis to it. Things like the use of the Theremin on the Beachboys

record, Good Vibrations, and even the Doctor Who theme. I was attracted to anything that had a kind of futuristic element to it. Even King Crimson, when they used the mellotron, it sounded very much like a Science Fiction soundtrack to me.

Of course, it's all wrapped up with TV and film. Things like 2001: A Space Odyssey, which blew my mind when I saw that film, and also watching the actual Space Race on the television. The moon landings and so on.

It was all part of the same thing. It was a particular moment in time when myself and my peers were all growing up through this "laying in the gutter but looking up at the stars," kind of way, in an almost literal sense, hoping that this unimaginable year of 2000 would be this fantastic era where everybody's flying around in "Jetsons" flying saucers and using jetpacks.

You've got to imagine that at that point, anything seemed possible because there were men walking on the moon. It literally did seem like anything was possible.

Anyway, all that futurism led to an appreciation of futuristic-sounding music for me. Obviously, groups such as Kraftwerk and Kraut Rock in general, all mixed up with Glam Rock, which was a big big thing in our house. (Brian) Eno in particular, I suppose, the ambient stuff. Loads of different influences. Very diverse, even some Disco.

Giorgio Moroder played quite a big part in my musical appreciation in my life. He is regarded as the father of disco and electronic dance music (which isn't bad for someone born in 1940 is it?), but he also pioneered a lot of electronic techniques that people still use today. He was so experimental! It did get me interested in playing myself. But I tried with guitar first. I actually bought a guitar with one of my first wage packets. I bought a Gibson SG copy for 30 quid, second-hand. I tried learning the guitar for a while but it hurt my fingers so I didn't fancy that. Also, what I found was, as with any traditional instrument, I was never very keen on the idea of learning the method of learning how to read traditional written music and doing scales and all that bollocks. I'm not really interested. So, for a while I put it on the back-burner.

Members of a local band, Caberet Voltaire, were friends with myself and others in my circle, and every year they had a big garden party at their parent's house. The one, absolutely epiphanic moment in my life, was when I heard a particular Kraftwerk song. I'd already heard some early Kraftwerk by then, and that all was on the "play list", and I found it a bit wet. It was a bit like flimsy Tangerine Dreamy, drifty hippy stuff and I wasn't that mad about it. But then they put on Trans-Europe Express at high volume with the big bass really pumping out – and to be honest, it completely blew my mind. I thought, "I want to do this." That was the moment when I thought, "I don't know if I can actually do it, but if I could do anything then this is the kind of music I'd like to create."

I'd given up on the guitar, and I was much more interested in creating sounds rather than music, and Cabaret Voltaire have always been kind of like that. Always playing around with effects and attempting to generate interesting sounds. It's really fascinating, because although I never wanted to make music like theirs, I did love that punk attitude ■ that

kind of "just go and do your thing, whatever it is..." attitude. So, inspired, as soon as the entry-level, affordable synths came out (which was, fortuitously, round about that exact time), I jumped in and bought one. You didn't need any traditional musical expertise at all to play around on those, and that was good as I had none!

The process of music is a lot different when you work with synths - the fact that right from the start, everything I did was put directly onto tape which you could alter as you saw fit, was important, rather than the traditional way of song writing - jamming in a rehearsal room for weeks, and then eventually recording what you've rehearsed.

The creative process was literally a building process. Right from the outset, I learnt things such as using multi-track recording and tape manipulation and a certain kind of assemblage of sounds and then editing the results. It's a different technique entirely. We basically took the production side of music from the end of the record to the beginning. It was a new way of working.

It was just a kind of experimental thing for me at that point, I was playing around with techniques without ever imagining that it would ever come to anything. It was just fun. You didn't need to know any music theory, but what you did need is an ear for a melody, an ear for sound, which I've always had - It was a perfect marriage.

My Friend Ian Marsh (who would later join The Human League and Heaven 17) had also bought a synth. And we could learn from each other. Then we started getting a little bit more serious. We began creating some good stuff

You were making music without an audience though? At some point you knew you had to have a stage act?

Yes, it did occur to us – this was the days before we could "share things online" of course! I had joined a creative arts youth club in the Holly buildings round the back of the City Hall called "Meat Whistle" in Sheffield. That was where I originally met Glenn Gregory and Ian Marsh and a load of my long-term friends that I still keep in contact with and work with to this day. That was kind of a safe environment for us to try things out in front of your friends. There were about 50 or 60 of us.

We created some demos and hauled them around the record companies. They all said, "This is terrible!" apart from Virgin and Island Records, who showed some interest, but they said, "Go away and write some tunes!"

Basically, what they meant was, "Write some pop songs! Come back to us when you've written some stuff that we can use." We were a bit deflated – we had a female singer at the time and she was good but not really what we were looking for. We needed someone that had a better look and image. Someone a bit more striking and unusual. And that's when I remembered my best mate at school - Phil Oakey.

I got in touch, and he sounded interested – I did say at the time that "He looks great but I don't know if he can sing." We gave him the backing track to Being Boiled, which myself and Ian had just written and said, "Could you try and write some lyrics to it?" and he obviously did. We loved it but we weren't sure about how the rest of the world would see it.

I played it to various friends, and to a guy called "Bob Last" who ran a record label in Edinburgh, and he loved it, which was a huge surprise to me. I said, "You can't be serious, nobody's going to want to listen to this. It's too mad." Next thing we know John Peel's playing it on his radio show, and we had four or five record companies showing interest in signing us!

We had meetings with companies such as Fiction Records. We were invited into an office with no furniture. We had to sit on the floor. They played us another song from a band that they were going to sign – The Cure – and we sat there listening to what would eventually be The Cure's first single (Killing an Arab) – in all honesty I thought it was rubbish, and so we eventually signed for Virgin.

Anyway, The Human League was born! From then on, we began to record music and tour.

David Bowie was in the audience one-night listening to The Human League and he was quoted as saying "I've just seen the future of pop music?"

Yes. Very nice of him to say so. He was right, really, in a way, in terms of how music evolved. There's a better story to that, actually. Unbeknownst to us, a month earlier we had played another gig, and for whatever reasons both David Bowie and Iggy Pop turned up at the door and got turned away by the bouncers.

When he DID actually see us, and when he was quoted as saying that, it was in a shit-hole pub and he just walked into the

dressing room unannounced to say hello. It was just amazing. Literally amazing, himself and his entourage. I've still got a photo of it to prove it happened!

Electronic music is often seen as a break-away from the "punk" music scene, but in a lot of ways was it just an extension?

The interesting thing was that we saw ourselves as more punk than punk because we were actually doing something radically different. Because of the age we were (we were probably a couple of years older than the people who initially got into punk) we'd seen it all before – we'd grown up through Glam Rock and seen bands such as The New York Dolls and the New York Punk scene, which we loved but it was nothing new to us.

When the British punk came along, and there were some fantastic bands. My personal favourite was The Damned. Myself and my friends actually were punks for about three weeks, but we soon got bored with it because we thought, "If you want to do something radical then do something REALLY new, because for all of punks posturing, it really was just rock and roll, really, isn't it?" It was rock and roll under a new hat. It's the same old same old and we wanted to be the future.

The only way we could do it was to set ourselves a "manifesto" - we basically, wanted to break away from the traditional approaches, and so we decided that there were to be no guitars and no songs about love. Well... not overtly about love. We've always been big fans of a restricted palette. It makes you more creative.

We wanted to carve ourselves a niche that was different to everybody else really, we saw ourselves at the time as being "electronic punk". We only had two synthesizers and a microphone and a tape recorder. That was it until we got signed with a proper record label. Then we moved into the multitrack territory. We wrote the demos for our first album The Luxury Gap on an Akai keyboard with a port-a-studio built in.

We literally wrote Let me go, Temptation, and Come live with me on a kind of Neanderthal version of a digital audio work station. Again, the limitations made you do things in a different way because you only had a limited number of sounds. You had to focus on the actual impact of the chordal sequences and melodies, because the sounds weren't very sophisticated.

You split from Human League to form Heaven 17, didn't you?

Yes. But I had no hand in it. Human League were going to be fantastic – we all knew that. But I just turned up at the studio one day and our manager was there and said, "We're throwing you out of the band, Martyn."

Just like that.

I remember saying, "Why?" Of course, I was gobsmacked. I had no warning. It turned out, in the fullness of time that it was all a fait accompli, contrived by our management and the record company to try and get the two bands for the price of one, fundamentally. I just converted my feelings into anger and creative energy and I set about starting a new band.

The first thing I did was ring up Glenn Gregory. We'd been friends before I met Phil as I've mentioned before. Now the thing about Glenn is I thought he had an even "better look" than Phil Oakley who I still love and get on with by the way. But if Glenn had not moved down to London to find his fame and fortune about three months before we formed The Human League, he would have been the singer of the original Human League. He'd given up on London and had just moved back to Sheffield too. Fate often seems to work in your favour. I thought, "How can we make this different and better than the Human League?", so we had a meeting.

We thought that the "limited palette" approach to the Human League, whilst sounding fantastic, would ultimately lead to songs becoming samey and stale, so we decided all bets were off in terms of restricting ourselves

instrumentation wise. We could now use guitars (a bass and a lead guitar). We could have used real drums if we'd wanted to, but we preferred the sound of the new drum machines. It sounded more futuristic, and I could program it as well - so even better!

We were partying to lots of black American imported dance records. So, we thought, why don't we make something like that? Even if we can't do it properly, because we don't have the expertise, at least what comes out will sound interesting, if we're aiming for that. The key to finding that distinct sound was finding John Wilson, the bass player. He was just a genius. So, we had a new sound and it worked.

Did you think that unique sound of Electronica became mainstream too quickly?

Absolutely – it was popular, and other types of music had to evolve to incorporate it. Pop caught up with the technology as did all other types of music.

Over time any form of music has to evolve to survive. But as I said before, Heaven 17 had evolved from the minimalist approach for this exact same reason, and not just to sound different to The Human League. The restrictions you give yourself become a problem too. I think that the bands that stuck with it haven't evolved and it shows.

A case in point is Kraftwerk. Now, I love Kraftwerk, and I've seen them several times. It is a fantastic "pony", but it is a "one-trick pony". It managed to make a 50-year career out doing the same thing. I think they found a niche and they're absolutely flogging that horse to death. They've been touring with the same show now, more or less, for decades. Don't you think you'd get bored? I know it's earning plenty of money, but I just don't see the point because they don't even do that much on stage. They might as well be replying to their emails. You know, the irony is, in the late '70s, at one point they did a few gigs where they had robots on stage taking their places, instead of them…

I'm not criticizing them. They are providing entertainment to a lot of people around the world, but it's like just a money-generating thing.

A *more aggressive sounding genre of Electronica had emerged – so-called "Industrial Music" – Pioneered by Throbbing Gristle and Gary Numan. What did you think of that style of music?*

I thought Gary Numan's records sounded great. I loved them but we were annoyed at the same time. Don't get me wrong – we had our share of success, but after his records were hitting the charts, I was completely pissed off, as you can imagine, because we'd been flogging our asses around. We had been touring with Siouxsie and the Banshees, and Iggy Pop, and The Stranglers and all sorts of people, trying to build up an audience for that sort of music. And then Gary Numan's record goes straight to the Number One.

I felt like we were being ripped off a bit. It sounds a bit like a pastiche of what we were trying to do. I'll actually admit that Cars is a fantastic record. But we're mates with Gary Numan. It's fine. Good luck, son. You did exceptionally well, and you wrote some great songs.

H *eaven 17 had a lot of hit records, but it sort of tailed off a bit – what happened after that?*

W e got dropped by Virgin, but we never split up. It never ended. In fact, we've been touring nonstop for the last 20 years. We've released loads of albums as well. It's never really stopped. We took a hiatus for a while, while I did my production work with people like Terence Trent D'Arby and Erasure, and B.E.S. and all that stuff.

How do you find working with other bands?

I'm not really super keen on working with bands. There's always too much politics involved. You know, the drummer hates the guitarist, all that malarkey, and there's cliques and all that stuff. I can't be doing with it.

I made a decision quite early on just to work with solo artists and put together bands around them or musicians around them and do the more traditional interpretation of what a producer should do, which is more like the 60s version of a producer. It's very easy just to plug individual singers into a certain style, which I create from scratch.

What do you think of the way modern music is developing?

I think it is very broken. There are plenty of great musicians out there, but no one wants to nurture them. The problem started in the late '80s when the marketing people started taking over and interfering with the creative process. People such as Simon Cowell began to evolve.

They thought they knew better than the artists and started to use marketing data to dictate how to make records. Fast-forward that over 30 years, and you end up with a much-reduced gene pool and a much narrower ecosystem of ideas. A&R department doesn't really exist anymore in the major labels.

It's all metrics and demographics and profit and loss projections. There are very few companies that run on gut instinct anymore. You know, the days when we were in the '70s and '80s when there was a kind of buzz about a band,

you'd invite a few A&R men down, and then every A&R man would turn up and all of a sudden there is a vibe about this amazing band. That shit, that happens less and less now.

I'm not even being cynical. It's how they actually do it. They sit in an office all day analysing what the existing market should look like. They care more about people that already have expose on TV than musical talent.

Let's assume somebody played something on the guitar on Celebrity Big Brother - that somebody would stand more chance of getting signed up to a record label than the most talented equivalents of Stevie Wonder. It's an extreme example, but that's why we ended up where we are.

I feel so sorry for any young, talented song writers. All these younger optimistic guys and girls need some help. They need to know how to make a career out of what they're doing. It breaks my heart a lot of the time to tell them the reality of the situation... to be honest, you are better off trying to get on some TV talent show". Things just die on the vine now, don't they? It's so sad.

I think Instant access to music has ruined people taking the time to appreciate music.

I agree, yes. The biggest problem, and I said this 15 years ago, the biggest problem about the digital proliferation of music is the artistic de-conceptualization of the music. We started the trend with CDs and then the idea of random access and then, of course, streaming music, which has just killed it stone-dead. The idea that record collections define your personality is gone now.

I've got a vivid memory of my daughter, when she was around eight years old. I'd bought her an iPod, and she'd been given a load of recordings of mine on there, in a folder called "Daddies songs" or whatever...

She was playing them to her friends on a little speaker. I was listening to what they were playing. They would just literally play 10 seconds of then song then move on something else. Not just my songs – there were others on there. It's the ultimate de-contextualization. They didn't know who it was a lot of the time, they didn't care who it was, or when it was made, what the artwork was, what the original artistic intention was. I'm not being judgmental, it's just a sad denudation of meaning.

That's where you end up with - but a good thing in terms of being a consumer is you can listen to anything you want anytime you want. It's a Library of Alexandria of music at your disposal in your pocket.

The traditional music industry, it just feels really broken to me. I find it less interesting. I still love creating music, obviously and there are many, many more contexts in which music can be used now so, yes. I can't imagine anything worse than retirement though, to be honest. I have some collaborative ideas up my sleeve. I'll keep you posted.

A L I E N

I first saw Alien a few years after its initial release (I was only 10 years old in 1979) but I do remember seeing the chestburster scene on "Film '79" late one night and it terrified me. This is probably why ten-year olds shouldn't be allowed to babysit.

When I later saw the entire film in my teens, it made a lasting impression upon me. The design of the alien craft is extraordinary, and it rightly stands as a landmark film in both the science fiction and horror genres.

Brian Johnson

Brian Johnson has contributed to the special effects on many classic TV shows and films. Not only did he supervise the work on Alien, but later worked on The Empire Strikes back, The Neverending Story, and Dragon Slayer.

What was your childhood like?

I was born in Esher, in Surrey, in June '39. Just in time for the war! Actually, my mum said I'd caused World War 2! We lived near the Thames, in Sunbury. A short distance from Kempton Park POW camp. My father worked at Vickers Armstrongs building bombers for the airforce – Wellingtons and Warwicks and other Vickers designs. He worked in the same building as Barnes Wallis, the guy that invented the "Dam Buster" bombs.

Family life was average. The exciting times were when aircraft flew over the house at low altitudes on approach to Hanworth Air Park or Heston Airfield.

As kids of three-years-old, we could identify most of the aircraft that flew over.

Describe your family background?

It was the era where fathers expected you to be seen and not heard. My father was very staid. My mum tried to make up for it by smothering me in kindness which was often claustrophobic in intensity.

But my Father did take me to air shows after the war, and from that I had an interest in making models from balsa wood with rubber band powered propellers. I made planes, helicopters, and gliders, though mostly unsuccessfully! I did consider joining the RAF when I was a child, but I was in the air show crowd at the Farnborough air show when the DH 110 crashed and killed 31 people. That made me rethink wanting to become a pilot.

Your model making obviously got more and more ambitious?

Yes, I was a very keen amateur modeller, like a lot of children from that era. TV hadn't really taken off, and people had to have hobbies. I was fortunate enough to live very close to Les Bowie – who is generally regarded as the "Godfather of British Special Effects". When I first met him, he was working on the models for "The Dam Busters" movie that was in production. I supplied him with the blue prints for the Lancaster's from my book "Jane's All the World's Aircraft". Actually, I realised having seen Lancaster's close up that the plans weren't all that accurate but fortunately no one that saw the film seemed to notice!

Later I got the job (through Les), of sweeping the floor at Anglo-Scottish Pictures in Addlestone in a converted Church hall. I learnt how to load 35mm film into various camera magazines, Mitchells, Arri, Evemo, Newman Sinclair and others.

I left eventually to work for a company called Lintas but then got called up to do my National Service in 1959. I was in the RAF for two years, working on ground-based instrument landing systems. In Sylt, Germany, and RAF Benson. I left in 1961 and contacted Les again, who hired me to work with him on "The Day the Earth Caught Fire" – I was doing mist and fire effects, photo cut-outs and creating the mattes.

Once that film was completed, I worked at Hammer films, and I created lots of smoke, flame and rain effects. Derek Medics was a guy that had been trained by Les to create Matte paintings, and he was working with me there at Bray Studios, when he decided to go and work for Gerry Anderson on his "Four Falls" work. I hated puppets! However, when Gerry started to work on shows such as "Supercar" at the Anderson Studios on Ipswich Road, in Slough, I joined them, as I needed the money. And I worked on Stingray and Thunderbirds.

Your Career enabled you to work on so many classic Science Fiction TV series and films. Did you have a love of the genre when you were growing up?

Yes, one of my uncles ran a pub in Hampton-on-Thames, and when I stayed with him, I used to delve into his extensive library. That was the first time I came across science fiction books – some of the early classics such as HG Wells' War of the Worlds, and Jules Verne's 20,000 leagues under the sea, plus several short story books. It had me hooked.

I later discovered a book called "The Stars My Destination" by Alfred Bester which I adored.

You've worked on so many brilliant films but Alien specifically stands out as a masterpiece. How did the job of special effects director on the project come about?

I had cut my teeth in special effects on a lot of Gerry Anderson projects, obviously.

I was working on a pilot film for a new Gerry Anderson project called "Into Infinity" (the pilot film was completed but the series was never made), at Bray Studios and I was waiting for Season 2 of Space: 1999 to begin filming.

I got a phone call from Peter Beale (then European boss of Twentieth Century Fox), who asked if some USA executives could visit to check out the studio next week? They were looking for a place to film a new movie. Of course, I said "yes"!

We then had confirmation that Space: 1999, Season 2 was "green lit", and we began preparations. When the "Fox" executives arrived, and they saw our filming techniques, and asked us why weren't shooting using "Motion Control?" (This is, much as it sounds, you actually control the motion of a camera precisely

which means you can repeat the shot as many times as you like, but change the elements you are filming, and later composite everything into one segment of film). I explained that that method was a time intensive way of filming, and because we had to do around five shots a day, it was a non-starter. All of the shots we took were on original negative film, multiply exposed to avoid any optical printer combinations.

Two of the USA Fox executives (none other than George Lucas and Gary Kurtz) asked me to work on their new movie – they explained it was a science fiction movie. I said I couldn't as I had just signed up to work on Space: 1999 for another season.

They said "That's OK" and said they were working on a lot of "space" movies, and I could work on the second one instead. The first movie that they had offered me became "Star Wars".

So, after completing the work for Gerry Anderson, I met up with Peter Beale at Fox's offices in Soho Square, and met with Gordon Carroll, David Giler and the Director of Alien who was then Walter Hill. I was given a script and asked to budget the special effects work.

Gerry Anderson was also asked to attend, because Gerry had a merchandising company – Century 21 Merchandising. They would talk to him after I explained how I would do the "chest burster" sequence, and also how we would put together the various vessels, such as the refinery etc.

Eventually Gerry wasn't involved, as he wanted to be the visual effects producer, and they already had someone in that role, so eventually I received a letter of confirmation to be the special effects director on the movie.

What did you think of the original Giger concept art when you first saw it?

Giger designed the alien elements in the movie, including the vessels, and even the alien planet landscape. Giger based the designs on his book of surreal art "Necronomicon". I thought, like most people, that the artwork he produced was both beautiful but incredibly disturbing. Perfect for a horror film. He was a very engaging but weird person. He did have a very dry sense of humour, and was a gifted Jazz pianist. He had the bones of his first wife hanging from an oak beam in his living room.

I remember his handshake – it was like a cold floppy dry slab of steak. But he loved red wine, though it had to come from a good vineyard.

Ron Cobb, and Chris Foss produced the designs for the terrestrial ships, external and internal – they were a lot more traditional in style. "Mobius", the French comic book artist also helped out, and he did the fantastic designs for the space suits. Sculptors Peter Voysey and Dick Budden created the actual scenes from plasticine.

The biggest problem we had was scale. The ships were big, but there were limitations to what we could physically build. The "Space Jockey" sculpture was built actual size of course, but the elevator carrying the three crew members down to the surface didn't look large enough, so we had to cheat a bit there. We built some half-sized space suits and put children in them, to make the sets look twice the size. Ridley Scott's son was in one of the suits.

The model ships were fairly large – the Nostromo was 16 feet long.

How did you get the Alien egg to look so convincing?

Well it was made of fibreglass, and was semi-transparent. Ridley Scott actually had his hand wiggling in a rubber glove inside it to show movement. And we had literally gallons of KY Jelly that we poured over everything. We used oysters and other shellfish to make the insides look impressively gloopy – anything we could find really – sheep's stomach linings – things like that. We opened it using wires. The rest of it was down to clever filming angles.

The Chestburster scene is incredibly iconic

Yes – we used a full-sized pretend body for John (Hurt), which we laid on the table, and John patiently sat underneath the table (drinking whisky) – so his arms and head are visible, but the rest is a prosthetic. Obviously, this has become part of film folk-lore now, but we didn't tell the actors that the body was fake or what was going to happen, as Ridley wanted genuine surprise. But they knew something was going on because we had plastic sheets covering anything electrical.

I think the surprise came from the actual explosion of blood. Veronica Cartright (who played Lambert) gets a face full of it, and reacts rather badly to it – that was genuine shock!

We filmed the actual "last dinner" part AFTER we filmed the chestburster scene, a few days later. So, we had to clean the set up so it looked spotless, and then John reappears and they all have lunch. We filmed the scenes in reverse.

The model ships were amazing. Very gothic.

Yes, but The Nostromo was not my design though – we built it as a team, and it was the combined work of a few people. The artist Ron Cobb was involved and Ridley Scott had a lot of input in the model designs too.

Once we had the general shape, I didn't want to go ahead and make the big model until I knew exactly what it was going to look like. Ridley had a tendency to change things – Which is OK – he's a perfectionist.

What we did was – we made a model that was just over a foot and a half long – about 16-inches, I think. Quite detailed. I would take the "current" model down to Shepperton where the film was being shot (we ourselves were working in a different unit at Bray Studios, where we would make and then film the models), and show Ridley. And he would point out the changes he wanted. I waited until he'd asked for about a dozen

changes and by then we had an idea for the ship that was stable enough to go ahead and take the plunge to make the big models.

We did this for all of the ships. The big ships have metal mounts inside them so we could move them around – they were incredibly heavy and had to be strong. The bases of them were plywood, and then we would add detail – usually

things from Airfix model kits that we could cannibalise, just to give the big ships lots of interesting wickets and towers. Ridley would still ask for more detail – he wanted more antennae to stick out of the front for example, but later on, he dispensed with much of the detail on the actual refinery model, wanting a slightly simpler design.

It was an amazing film. Were you pleased with the end results?

Absolutely – a lot of people worked on the effects, and the combined effort won an Oscar. I left just before the movie was completed, as I was whisked away to work another Fox movie – The Empire Strikes back. And changes were still being made after I left, but It did look amazing.

I was lucky enough to go on to work on lots of other movies, such as The Neverending Story, DragonSlayer, and of course, Aliens.

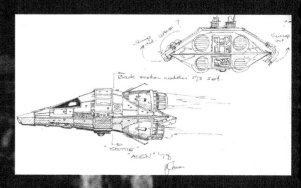

Sharpes
Novels

I have always, as long as I can remember, been interested in historical warfare, especially the eras when armies moved around in neat rows or squares, and wore elaborate uniforms. Or sea battles where you had to fight it out toe-to-toe with an opponent. I was interested in anything from Ancient battles right up to the start of World War 1, when everyone realised that maybe hiding in holes and trenches was a good idea, and they could fire at their enemies over the horizon.

I love reading the actual histories, but I also love the novelisation of those battles too, and not many caught my imagination like the Sharpe series of book, which were set in the Peninsula Wars against Napoleon, and the hero was Richard Sharpe, a working class (mostly) believable protagonist.

Bernard
Cornwell

Bernard Cornwell wrote the Sharpe series, and also several other favorites of mine, from a fabled pre-historic time of King Arthur, through the Saxon and Viking eras, English Civil War, and the American Revolutionary War.

Can you remember the first book that really made an impression upon you?

I simply don't remember! Sorry! It was probably some ghastly religious book as I was adopted into a family of evangelical fundamentalists. We read the bible every day around the breakfast table, which did at least give me a solid grounding in good prose, expanded my vocabulary and bored me rigid.

I am a big fan of the Hornblower books, like yourself. What did you like about them?

I think it's the character of Hornblower himself that is the major appeal, though of course we should never forget that Forester was a marvellous constructor of plots. Hornblower is such a decent and honourable man, and so prey to self-doubt, that it's hard not to want to spend time in his company. The odd thing is that Forester himself was often reluctant to write another book about Hornblower. The tale is told that the great editor Angus Cameron used to be despatched to California with a

bag full of whiskey and told not to return to the office until he'd persuaded Forester to write another Hornblower. We should all be grateful to Angus Cameron!

You seem to gravitate towards European history? Why do you think that is?

I'd say I gravitated towards British history – because we're always advised to 'write about what you know' and, being born, educated and raised in England I know British history best. And British history is what I was brought up with, as well as being of general interest to me too. It is a long history, and this gives me a lot of scope to focus on certain "ages" too.

You obviously do a lot of research before writing the books. How much time do you spend before you leap into writing?

How about a lifetime? Research is a lifetime project – meaning that for years I read history and much of that reading forms the bedrock of knowledge which informs the books. It's almost impossible to say how much research is needed, it totally depends on the book you're writing. I plainly have a great deal of useless knowledge about the Napoleonic Wars and the Anglo-Saxon period, so the specific research for any one novel can be done fairly fast, in, say, a couple of months, if not less. But when I tackle a period that is outside of those areas it does take longer. I wanted to write a novel about Shakespeare's theatre and I suspect I read deeper and deeper into that period and subject for about three years. The only time I've ever set aside a period (six months) to research a subject was when I wrote the Arthurian trilogy (The Winter King, Enemy of God and Excalibur) and got so bored

with it that after three months I abandoned the research and start writing. Which worked. But of course, you go on researching while writing.

Do you think you can sometimes do too much research? How much research do you typically have to leave out in order to make a story a good one?

You can't do too much research, but you must learn what to leave out. I guess I abandon 95% of my research. Our job is NOT to bore the reader! I write dramas from within history, and I do have to keep the history part as accurate as I can, but sometimes, if it is something minor, I can deviate a little, or merge two very minor historical characters into one, just to make the stories less convoluted and more entertaining. Where this happens, I usually make a note at the back of the book explaining the decision though.

You're first book was a Sharpe novel. Why did you choose the Napoleonic era for it?

Because I desperately needed to make some money! An ignoble motive, but there it is. I had a proper job as a television producer when I met an American and fell madly, wonderfully in love. Judy couldn't live in Britain because of pressing family reasons and I really didn't have any close ties so said I'd move to the States. The American government, in its infinite wisdom, refused me a green card so I airily told Judy I'd write a book. Ha ha.

It occurred to me that Hornblower, Bolitho and Ramage were all making their creators a decent living and I wondered why no one had tried the same with

Wellington's army instead of Nelson's navy, and so that's what I chose. I thought there'd be readers who'd want those stories and so it proved. The better news is that forty years on we're still married.

Do you think your depiction of Sharpe has evolved over time? Has Sharpe mellowed?

I suppose he has? I really don't know as I never re-read early books. I do know that if I start a book with the word 'Sharpe was in a good mood' it won't work. I hope he hasn't mellowed! I intend to write one more Sharpe book and it will be interesting, after a long gap of ignoring him, to see how he behaves. Not well, I hope.

Your heroes always seem to have a sidekick. Do you think you need these to balance your leading characters?

Certainly not for balance – but to give a hero a sidekick gives him someone with whom he can talk on a different level to anyone else in the book, and as I'm a great believer in dialogue being incredibly useful as a way of imparting information to the reader and propelling the plot, that's extremely useful.

Your Saxon era books are a particular favourite of mine. The history from this period is often hazy due to lack of records and the sheer number of smaller kingdoms. Did you find this challenging when planning the books?

If anything, it's liberating! If you write about a period for which the historical record is detailed and voluminous then, to an extent, you're bound by the real history. Obviously, as a novelist,

you can make things up, but the historical background must be authentic and so you can't have real-life characters swanning off to some place they never visited – i.e. you can't suddenly invent Wellington campaigning in Italy. If the historical record is scanty then all bets are off. I can never decide which is easier to write, a book informed by meticulous historical sources, or a book set in an undocumented period. I guess the latter? I'm amused by the assumption that I plan the books. I wish I could!

Do your publishers keep in constant touch, or do they leave you mostly alone when you write?

The publishers leave me well alone until I submit the manuscript (when I actually press 'Send' on the computer) and then the editing process starts, other than that we stay good friends and if they ever ask how a book is going, I say 'fine' regardless whether it is or not. We've worked together for a long time, and trust on both sides is strong.

Are there any current historical fiction authors that you really admire?

Hilary Mantel is a goddess, and I read everything that C.J. Sansom writes – he's wonderful! Of course, I read mostly factual history books, as I need to constantly research for the books I write, but I do have occasional leisure time too!

How do you feel about downloadable books? Weren't Amazon attempting to lower the price of Kindle books, for example?

I have no idea about Amazon and Kindle. I take the view that cheaper books are good and will sell in greater volume. I adore downloadable books! I download onto an iPad and read there, but if I really like a book, I'll also buy it in hardback – recently I did that for Tara Westover's marvellous memoir, Educated, and for Stephen Greenblatt's Tyrant.

Are you happy?

I am, thank you!! Couldn't be happier!

TERRY PRATCHETT

Discworld Novels

Terry Pratchett books came into my life much later than they should have done. I was already a big fan of satire – and Terry's Discworld Novels were a long series of very funny books, that parodied the fantasy genre of literature mercilessly before they settled down a bit and went on to create their own wonderful universe.

Amy Kingston Anderson

The artist who created the covers did a great job of setting the mood of the books – mysterious and funny, and often chaotic, light hearted but with dark undertones.

Sadly, both Terry Pratchett and Josh Kirby had passed away by the time I'd started to write this book, but I chatted to Josh's niece – Amy Kingston Anderson, and she gives us a fascinating glimpse of what Josh was like as a person.

You knew Josh Kirby since you were very young of course, but what is your first memory of him?

That is such a hard question because he's been in my memory since I can remember. I know a very vivid memory that I have from being very young, maybe seven or eight, is going to visit him on school holidays, and getting to the front door and just being so excited to see him and the anticipation of waiting for him to open the kitchen door (we never went in the front door) with his lovely smile.

Going to visit him was always my favourite and best adventure, because I was allowed to go and roam the house on my own, He lived in this large old Tudor rectory of many rooms, and with an attic full of interesting things. There were sections of it that hadn't been touched in years before he moved there, and which he would leave alone, which was wonderful, because when walking through the house, it felt like you were ducking into time warps…walking into frozen moments of history.

I was allowed to roam free, sometimes to the point where I would actually get lost. I had to knock on the floor and yell until someone found me! Really fantastic times.

Each room was filled with his paintings, hanging on the walls, and some of them literally stacked up on the floor against the walls and in massive chests.

He seems like such an interesting character - What was he like as a person?

One of the kindest people I have ever known. I think he didn't have a mean bone in his body. Shy, especially with people he didn't know, but always warm and kind. A sharp sense of humour though - his eyes were always twinkling - you could always tell that he was seeing the fun and whimsy in anything that he looked at. I don't think he looked at things the same way that others did. That shows up in his work. Everything has this wonderful air of the fantastic, and humorous.

He was extremely generous. Both with his time and his care of others. Art students and children creating art projects would write to him often – they would be doing their thesis on him, or wanting to ask him questions about fantasy art and art in general. And he would personally answer every single letter he got. He would have students actually turn up at his door to show them their work and he would always spend a lot of time with them and show

them around his own workshop and talk about art. He was very passionate about the importance of art in the world, art in school and art as something that was vital to the development of mankind. So, even though he was a quiet spoken man, his kindness spoke volumes.

Where did he create his art?

He had built a two-story studio space in one section of the house so that he could paint his larger pieces, because some of the pieces he painted were up to five feet tall. But funnily enough he rarely used it. The only time he would use it is was when he was painting something really large.

For all the rest of his work, he painted in what was the pantry off the main kitchen and little living/ dining room area. It was tiny, literally the size of a broom cupboard, but it had the best light in the house – north light, which is the cleanest, purest light, he said.

which very quickly turned into what became his magnum opus, painted over 30 years. So, yes, that's what he did. He painted. And then occasionally he would pop down to see his family for a roast dinner on a Sunday.

He was an artist, and I think that there is eccentricity in anyone who creates art, and imagines new worlds with infinite possibilities. I think people may think he was eccentric because of how passionate and dedicated he was to creating art, even though he also was an extremely sensible and level headed person.

He did have this one thing that didn't totally fit in with the quintessential concept of an eccentric painter - he drove a red sports car - a Porsche! And refused to wear a seatbelt! He actually had managed to arrange a doctor's note, in the '60s before it became legal to have to wear a seatbelt, which said he was exempt from wearing one!

So, this wonderful artist in his jeans with a hole in the back pocket, because he'd sit on his wallet until it would wear right through, and a denim shirt and fisherman's jumper, would drive everywhere in a red sports car with no seatbelt!

There was basically only enough room for an easel, his chair, and shelving on one side that was stacked to the ceiling with hundreds and hundreds of scraps of magazines, newspapers and reference material for whatever he was working on at the time, interspersed with his sketches.

There was a human skull propped in there somewhere. Don't ask me where he got it, I don't know to this day…. and a radio - and that was it.

Was there a special part of the day when he worked?

Josh worked all day, every day because he didn't consider it work. It was his absolute life's passion. It is what he felt that he was born to do. At a young age in school when everybody was asked to create a sign describing what they wanted to do when they grew up, Josh wrote, "Artist."

So, he would literally wake up at dawn so that he could start painting as soon as the sun came up, and he would paint throughout the day with a quick break for lunch until the sun went down again, at which point he would have tea and go to bed.

He felt that music was a distraction while painting, although I know that he did love the Beatles very, very much. He definitely loved music, just not while working. While painting, he would listen to BBC Radio 4 as he felt that talking was far less distracting than music.

What were his interests outside of art?

If asked, "what do you do on your holidays, Josh?" He would say, "I paint." If he wasn't painting something commissioned (book cover, film cover, puzzle, privately commissioned piece etc.) He would paint for his own amusement.

And that's why we have such gorgeous and epic series such as the "Voyage of the Ayeguy" - that started off as a commissioned piece for an American poster portfolio and

What sort of things did you do together?

I'd come over and we would sit at his tiny little dining room table, and drink very weak tea and eat large amounts of burnt toast with marmite, and I would ask him about art and what he thought about certain things. I would always bring the books I was reading (that were always either science-fiction or fantasy books) so I could show him the covers and we'd talk about them. And he was so wonderful because he would never say a bad word about them.

He would ask me what I thought, and ask me to explain the things that I thought were wonderful, and the things that were possibly weak about them. We had some really amazing conversations.

One of my most beloved possessions in life is that for one Christmas, he gave me a book of Grimms' fairy tales illustrated by Arthur Rackham (which was one of his favourites). It's one of the lovely versions with tissue paper in between each of the illustrated plates. So lovely.

Are you artistic?

Yes. Now I've grown up, I'm primarily a performing artist. I was trained as a classical ballet dancer and I work in theatre and the performing arts. I also inherited the "fine art" gene. There are a couple of us in the family. My mum was also a fine artist.

Josh was a constant form of inspiration throughout my life and always extremely encouraging of what I was doing. I remember when I'd finished my A-level art exam and all of my projects were up and displayed for the examiners to go through, the thing that I was actually most worried about was making it look amazing because Josh was going to come and see it!

What do you miss about Josh the most?

Actually, I think the world misses his extraordinary, vibrant contribution to art and literature and visual storytelling. I have hundreds and hundreds and hundreds of instances of people saying, "I picked up A book or B book or C book because Josh's cover caught my eye and imagination." That is an unbelievable homage to what I think Josh gave the world through his art. So, from an artistic point, I miss that.

From a personal point of view, he was so kind and so twinkly and so wonderful, and I miss all of those things.

HOOTERS

I saw The Hooters when they played on Friday Night Live. I was in love with them immediately. They played Karla with a K, and Satellite – Melodic rock with folk leanings here and there. Exactly the sort of music I loved at the time. They never really made it big in the UK but I followed their careers closely, and still play their music.

Eric Bazilian

Lead singer and song writer, he fronted The Hooters brilliantly. He has also written a number of hit songs for a long list of other artists such as Cyndie Lauper and Robbie Williams.

Could you tell us a little bit about your early life, your upbringing?

Okay. I had a typically atypical upbringing in Philadelphia. My mother is a concert pianist. My father was a psychiatrist. So, I grew up surrounded by music and deep thought. Again, I thought it was typical. Apparently, my parents had a lot of odd friends, so I grew up surrounded by very interesting, unusual people.

My mother was the musical one, and played the piano. I was drawn to it, and started taking piano lessons at six, found that I didn't have the discipline nor the desire, really, to play classical music. Gave that up at seven or eight.

At nine, my uncle taught me some guitar cords. He was a folk musician. I performed on TV for the first time just after this. I performed a Joan Baez song on local TV. It was in Spanish. I learned El Preso Numero Nueve. Then, February 1964, age 10, I was one of the millions of young boys who saw The Beatles on The Ed Sullivan Show and my life was changed forever...

I looked at those guys and I said, "That's what I want to do." That really set the trajectory. Since I already had some facility in playing the guitar, I was able to start picking up their songs very quickly. I started my first band the next day with my friend Bernie, who, since he didn't play an instrument yet, decided he was going to play the drums.

The band was called The Limestones. I thought of that name because it was like "The Quarrymen" which was the name of "The Beatles" originally. The

band didn't get far though - we were only 11 and 12 years old and there's only so far you can get at that point.

I spent years looking for the right combination of people. The hardest thing was to find somebody who could really sing. Then, when I was 15, we found a young man who was 16, an older fellow, who not only could play really good rhythm guitar, he could sing amazingly and he wrote songs. We formed a band called Evil Seed, which was sort of "heavy metal". That was the first real band I had where we had real songs and real arrangements. At that point, we'd do a lot of covers of Cream, Hendrix, Jeff Beck, all the British blues rock that followed in the wake of The Beatles.

That took me through high school. Then, I went off to university at 18 because that's what you did back then. I tried studying music but wasn't particularly inspired by what they had to offer at the university I was attending.

I ended up getting a degree in physics, because I'd had this whole parallel life as a science geek. I was a ham radio operator from the time I was nine. I always built my own equipment. Before

The Beatles came along, I was going to be the first pre-pubescent kid in outer space.

Anyway, it was in my first week at university that I met Rob Hyman in an electronic music class where they had a synthesizer. I recognized him. He was in a band that was already getting some notoriety around Philadelphia, and we connected. I joined his band as a guitarist. That band was Baby Grand, and we produced two albums in, '77, and '78. We were either ahead of our time or behind our time, but it wasn't the right time – not for those records. It was sort of like Steely Dan on steroids.

Now, we're already up to 1979. We were trying to write a third album and we realized that this just wasn't the vehicle for us. The singer Rick Chertoff decided that he wasn't born to rock - which was true. He's a brilliant, brilliant writer, and he had a very distinctive voice, but was never comfortable being the front man in a rock band.

So, both myself and Rob had a go at singing and realised we weren't bad. This was right around the time that the second British Invasion was happening. We thought, "You know what? Let's do that! The world doesn't have to know that we are virtuoso instrumentalists. Let's dumb it down in a smart way and write some really cool ska and reggae songs," which we did. That takes us to 1980.

So why did you call the band The Hooters?

We were looking for a plural noun that was not a household object, so that everyone in the band could say, "I am a," not a shoe or a chair, but like a Beatle or a Rolling Stone. With this thought in the back of our minds, we went in to do our first demo recordings. We were getting set up – one of the instruments was a melodica - and the engineer said to us through the talk-back, he said; "Let me get a level on that hooter." So, the melodica became the hooter and it didn't take more than a couple of days for us to realize, "Hey, there's our plural noun that's not a household object." So, we became The Hooters, which really seemed like a good idea at the time. Had the restaurant chain not come along, it would have remained a good idea.

Your Success was quite sudden wasn't it?

It was. One of the recordings was a ska instrumental by Don Drummond called Man in the Street. Through happenstance, we ended up getting that recording played on a local radio station, WMMR, which supported local musicians back then. A disc jockey named Michael Pierson played it, and the phones went crazy, and the song went into regular rotation.

We sort of had a hit with it - a bizarre ska instrumental. All of a sudden, we went from playing five events a week at biker bars in the suburbs to playing clubs in

the city. Then, we did a residency every Monday night at this one club called Grendel's Lair. It was sort of like The Beatles at The Cavern. The first time we played we had 50 people in the audience, and then we had 70, and within a couple of months, the line was literally around the block.

How did the hooters write records? Did you share the responsibility?

It was absolutely not a democracy. It was a benevolent oligarchy. It was Rob and I that were the writers. That was the idea from the beginning, that we were the leaders of the band. The directors. We were open to suggestions from the other members of course. If somebody came in with a great idea, we were certainly all ears, but I think we had an identify from early on.

The first song that we wrote was, All You Zombies, which is probably the song that we're most universally known for. We didn't rate it very highly at first ourselves – we weren't confident at that time in our own song-writing abilities, and we would always start our first set with that song just to get it out of the way - it never occurred to us that anyone would actually like it. But they did. Not bad for a reggae themed bible story. That song eventually did become the first single. Even though it never did much in the charts – it reached number 57 in the US, (although it was number one in Australia), If I wanted to pick one song that really characterizes our band and our song writing, it would be that one.

You opened for The Who on the Farewell Tour?

Yes, we did. It was The Who, The Clash, Santana, and The Hooters. I have many photographs from that show. I was riveted. I had never seen anything that loud, that powerful, with that much visual information on stage at the same time. I felt myself looking at John Entwistle a lot because I got tired of watching Pete and Keith and Roger. They moved around way too much.

When we were back stage, I never dared to walk up to Pete for a chat, even though I really wanted to. He did not give off a vibe of, "Hey, come to talk to me!" Although since then, we have had e-mail communications. He always answers my e-mails and has complimentary things to say. I don't think that he really wants to hear me fanboy out on him though so much, so I try to keep that to a minimum. Well from touring with these heroes of ours we recorded our first album as The Hooters, which was "Nervous Night" which surprised us with its success. It sold 2 million albums across the world, and gave us hits with "Day by Day", "And we danced", as well as "Where do the children go?" with Patti Smith – Rolling Stone magazine named us "Best New Band of the Year" which was amazing.

Our next Album – One Way Home broke us in the UK where we had a big hit with "Satellite" and appeared on Top of the Pops, and Friday Night Live. Our video for Satellite had heavy exposure on the new MTV channel too, which really helped. In fact, we seem to have a lot of fans in the UK – I'd say more so than the USA actually. We seemed to have caught the imagination of the youth there.

It must have been daunting to play at Live Aid? How did you get invited to do that?

We opened the Philadelphia section. That was a last-minute coup on the part of our management and the local promoter in "Philly", Larry Magid, who just really believed that we deserved to be on that concert.

Sir Bob Geldoff wasn't so happy with that, apparently. In fact, he left us off the DVD. I think he just didn't feel that we had earned a right to be on the show at that point. The quote was; "Who the fuck are The Hooters?"

Ironically, a week after the Live Aid DVD came out, he had to open a show for us in Germany with the Boomtown Rats. He was our support band. That was hysterical. He was a bit sheepish that night. But you know what? It was his right. Live Aid was his baby. If he didn't want us on the DVD, then fair enough.

It was a crazy day. I barely remember it. We were on and off stage. We were on for literally 10 minutes, but apparently, a billion people saw us all over the world that day. They can never take that away from us. I have a big picture of it in my studio!

You've done a lot outside of the Hooters. You worked with Cyndi Lauper on some of her big hits... How do you find working with other artists?

Yes, we did that first album of hers She's So Unusual. We spent about a year with her working on that. It's like any kind of a relationship. You have your times when it's a love fest and then suddenly you disagree about something and the boxing gloves are on. Cyndi's a very dynamic person. You really didn't know what you were going to get from one minute to the next. When we resonated, it was amazing. Then she'd come back and say, "No, I hate it. It was all wrong. It's stupid, I hate it!"

So, there was a lot of back and forth on it, but great art can come from that. I think we made a record that was certainly ground-breaking. It wasn't a record that I would have made on my own. My instincts are much more rock orientated. I like dirtier guitars. She didn't want to make a rock record, she wanted to make a dance record. I think what we made was something eventually that totally defies categorization.

Interestingly, on her hit Girls Just Want to Have Fun, she originally swore she would never sing that song. She thought it was demeaning to women. We persevered, myself and Rob Hyman (also from the Hooters), as we believed in the song. But we had to come up with an arrangement that worked because we had tried everything else and we were running out of options.

We tried doing it as a rock song, we tried doing it like a Cat Stevens song. We tried doing it as a reggae song. We came in one day and we were talking about Come on Eileen, which was ubiquitous at that point, and who didn't love Come on Eileen? Really, that's just one of the most, if not the most, likeable records ever. She said, "Well, can we make it like Come on Eileen?".

I said, "Okay. Let's try this." I remember I had an 808-drum machine at the time, and I programmed in the kick drum from Come on Eileen, that boom-bah-dah, boom-bah-dah. Then I picked up my guitar... and we were off and running. A little four-track demo was made, and we had it, and then after that she would always say; "I always wanted to sing that song."

The album title is pretty appropriate. She is unusual. She's also brilliantly talented. Not always the easiest to work with, but usually worth it.

Of the songs that you've written which is your favorite?

Of the ones that people know, I hate to be obvious here, but I would have to say One of Us. It was a song that wrote itself, even though I was in this meditative state when I wrote it. I literally just sang it. I created a musical track because my then-girlfriend, (now-wife) asked me to show her how my four-track porta-studio worked. I'd been playing that guitar riff all day, so I built a little arrangement, a little track around it. Then she said, "Sing it," and I sang it. That's literally what came out. I listen back and I say, like, "Wow, what? What is this? What am I saying here?" I still wonder sometimes.

I realize that, in some ways, that the four minutes that it took me to sing that song, the lyrics in it perfectly sums up my world view.

What if God was one of us
Just a slob like one of us
Just a stranger on a bus
Trying to make his way home?

That was the whole story right there. It was just happenstance that we were making a record with Joan (Osbourne), because the next day I played the demo for Joan and Rick Chertoff (who has produced some of The Hooters albums). Rick looked up and he said, "Joan, you think you could sing that?" Joan sang it. It sounded perfect.

The song had found its voice and the voice had found its song. We were going to be hearing that for a very long time.

You've co-written songs with a lot of other big stars such as Robbie Williams?

Yes. He was great. This was the very beginning of his career. He had just left Take That and the label had sent him to us to see what we could do with him. I don't think they really believed in him at that point.

I remember a lot of talk from his record label about a "boy band refugee" and "having a short shelf-life" and they just wanted to get something out in a hurry before people forgot who he was. Desmond my producer and I had a small catalogue of songs and we thought we'd run it by Robbie and see what would be a good fit for him, but Robbie didn't want to hear them. He wanted to write his own music – which surprised me.

Old Before I Die actually started when Robbie and I were sitting in a room with a guitar. I had just bought this little special-effects box that could make a guitar sound like anything. It had all these pre-sets and I was scrolling through them and there was one called, "Generation." So, I was messing around and I'd started playing My Generation (from The Who of course!), and Robbie and I sang My Generation together, first verse and the chorus. The song is a youth rebellion song, young voices are better than old. Talkin' about "My Generation" …

At the end of that, Robbie looked at me and said, "Wouldn't it be great to write a song that says the opposite, something like "I hope I get old before I die?"

It was a good idea – so I tried it, and I sang "I hope I'm old… before I die." It sounded good. We had our chorus. We wrote that chorus in minutes and then Desmond came in, heard us singing, and said, "That's gold!"

We wrote the verses together and put the whole thing together. We actually did a full production of that but Robbie ended up re-cutting it with a different guitarist. Which was cool. It was his song too. But it was the first time I'd ever had a hit song that I hadn't played on, where I hadn't been a part of the final production. On the one hand, was a little off-putting because I was used to hearing my guitar on the record with the singer. But there was something very empowering about it too, knowing that I'd written a song and it was so good that it didn't need my guitar on it to be a hit.

He was delightful. He actually rang me later to see if we could work on some more records together, but for whatever reasons, it never happened again. I have great memories of working with him and I'm very proud of the artist that he became. I think he really rose above and beyond what people had expected of him…

And your career now?

The Hooters still tour. I live in Switzerland now, and so we tend to play in Europe more than any place else. Germany's the gift that keeps on giving, we seem to be very popular there. We tour at least a month there every summer in Germany. In the US, we mostly just play in Philadelphia now though. Although, now, we have this annual tradition where we play Disney World.

I don't think I'll ever stop. I've had a lot of different projects – I like to try new things all of the time, as well as my own solo work – I've also produced a Swedish horror rock band. I'm not saying that they're all going to be hits, but it's just these crazy, varied opportunities come up and it's too much fun to stop.

THE THING

Now regarded as a science fiction classic, The Thing is set around two polar science teams (the remains of a Norwegian one that are only in the story briefly), and an American team which comes up against an alien that can take over and imitate any lifeform. In the claustrophobic confines of a small set of living quarters and labs cut off from the rest of the world, it is a story of paranoia and survival. Who are the aliens? Who are The Things? Who can you trust? The answer is no one.

It features superb pre-CGI special effects from Rob Bottin, who was so traumatised by the experience that he never made another film.

Thomas Waites

Thomas Waites had been in lots of big-name films such as The Warriors, before he was given the role of "Windows" in The Thing...

You were raised in New York – How did you become an actor?

My first break I guess was getting into Juilliard acting school, because I had worked on a Romeo monologue for so many years by that point. I was a little obsessed with Shakespeare. I think I was 17 when I auditioned. I have such a connection with it, and I'm a great romantic. I'm always in love with somebody. They gave me a full scholarship. That was my first break and I thought, "Well maybe I have something. Maybe I have a chance."

But I got into a lot of trouble at school, got kicked out of Juilliard after three years. I was getting into fights – physical fights. I came from the sort of background in Brooklyn where fighting was common amongst boys my age.

Then, I was really on my own for a while. It's cold out there when you don't have any money, or any job, or any place to go. I starved and lived from couch to couch for

three months. And then fortune smiled - a director I had worked with at Juilliard by the name of Stuart Vaughan was kind enough to give me an introduction to a casting director by the name of Michael Fender.

Michael saw me and he saw that I could handle verse. He said, "You're surprising, because you don't look like you can handle verse and yet you can, and you do it splendidly. I'll submit you for some roles." He started submitting me and my first professional role was playing Red Ryder in When You Coming Back Red Ryder by Mark Medoff at the Center Stage in Baltimore. That's when I finally got my Equity card. I got my first agent too, and then I started getting movie roles – made for TV ones to begin with. I did a movie for PBS, Pity the Poor Soldier and then I did a movie called On the Yard. All of these led to me getting the role of Fox in The Warriors. Then I was off to the races after that. I'm like, "Well, I guess this is what I'm doing for the rest of my life." I was lucky.

You fell out with the director of The Warriors? What happened there?

I did fall out with the director, right. I was offered The Wanderers and The Warriors at the same time. I was at a sort of zenith moment in my career. I was 23.

Walter Hill the director on The Warriors, contacted me and said, "Hey, listen, why don't you come over to the office and watch Rebel Without a Cause?", because that's how I see your character in the movie. I said, "Great" I went in and I watched it. I said, "Yes, I really see this movie as a guy that turns away from violence, and finds romance." Walter said, "Well, that's exactly how I see it." In a

way it reflected what I was trying to do in my own life. So, based on that evaluation of the story, I agreed to do the movie. We got onto the set and things started to get very stressful. We got way behind in filming and we were way over budget.

Not only that, but the film was turning out to be a super violent movie, which of course now, is a freaking joke, compared to what movies are like today. It was like kindergarten compared to what's out there now. Anyway, it got on Walter's nerves that I was constantly asking questions and questioning his authority. He had bigger problems to worry about, I guess.

What I should have done is called my agent and said, "Listen, this is not working out the way we had planned and the way we had agreed. I need you to intercede on my behalf and go to bat for me.", but I didn't do that...

And filming was hell for us – the conditions weren't ideal. The first day of work, they put eight actors in one trailer in the stultifying New York City summer heat. Eight fucking guys getting changed in a 4 X 4 cell, basically. I was like, "Wait a fucking minute here. Wait a minute you guys, I don't mean to be difficult but you can't put eight guys in one trailer." So, then they gave us two trailers. But then, I became the official pain in the ass. And I was fired. I wish he hadn't had fired me. I wish he had just taken me aside and said, "Look, stop asking me so many questions or I'm going to have to fire you." Give me a warning. You don't have to fire a guy, because that's a tough thing to come back from. I wish he had been a bit more considerate in that regard, and not so harsh with me, because it really upset me.

When I saw the movie, I didn't like it and I didn't like the fact that I'd been fired. I was an angry young man. I was still in my early 20s. I said, "I want my name removed from the credits!", as if I were some big movie star. That pissed off Paramount and it pissed off Walter. I got to apologize to him later. I lost so many jobs because people thought I was difficult to work with. Although I tried to make it work for myself, - I concluded that I lacked discipline, so I ended up becoming a black belt in karate and went into psychotherapy. I really try to make it ultimately benefit me. I think that -getting fired, can ultimately make you a more interesting actor.

How did you get the part of Windows in The Thing?

I was starting to get roles again, and at the time, was in a hit production of a play called American Buffalo with Al Pacino. It was one of those deals where we had lines of people queuing around the block to see it. There were just three-character's in it. Myself, Al Pacino, and a great actor by the name of Clifton James. I guess, much to my surprise, Kurt Russell and John Carpenter were in town to cast The Thing, and they had come to see it too.

My agent called me the next day and said, "Listen, they want you to come in and read for this movie, The Thing. It's being directed by John Carpenter (who had just made a big name for himself with both Halloween and the Elvis Presley TV movie that he directed together with Kurt.)" I had been doing the play with Al for quite a long time by that point, so this was late July or August, so I was ready to do something else.

I went in to do the reading with John and Kurt, but in all honesty, I didn't think I was going to get the role - I hardly even prepared for the reading - I mean the character was Hispanic. His name was Sanchez actually, in the original script! I went in because I admired John Carpenter, and it was nice to meet him, and I read, and I walked out, and I never thought twice about it again. I thought, "Well, I definitely won't get that because I'm obviously not Hispanic." Anyway, my jaw hit the ground when they did actually offer me the part!

We shot it in '81 and I just had the greatest time of my life. We had such a blast, so much fun, it was just like a pot boiler of jocularity. From storytelling to pranks. We had two weeks of rehearsals before we started filming, which is very rare, and during that two weeks, we kind of bonded as a group. They took good care of us. They gave us great accommodation. It was one of the high points of my existence I have to say.

Did you get any input about how your character was shown in the film?

Not so much. But I created the nickname "Windows" for the character. After he was no longer going to be Hispanic, they dropped the name Sanchez, but then they called him John Simmons which I thought was really bland.

I wore these dark green glasses to rehearsal one day and I said to John Carpenter "I want everybody to call me "Windows" from now on. He laughed and said, "Windows......? All right." Not every cast member I think might have been pleased with that choice, but it ended up being hysterically funny. I mean, "Windows. Get away from there." It's just so bizarre and I admit to a certain extent, random, but still it was like I was trying to create some kind of character with some kind of depth. I think it worked out all right.

His style is, he is very relaxed. He likes to play games, he likes to have fun, but at the end of the day, he's really trying to tell a great story, a story that has some meaning, and some value, and depth to it. John is an interesting guy. He creates a very convivial environment on the set where everybody is free to let their personality out. Everybody is free to contribute. Everybody is, even at times, solicited for their observations or opinions, yet at the same time, make no mistake about it, he's the boss.

I

I was so disappointed that when the movie was released John did not get the accolades that he deserved for making what I thought was a darn good movie.

Do you think the film was hampered by the trend at the time to show aliens as peaceful and friendly – "Close Encounters" had been released a few years earlier, and The Thing was released in the same week as E.T. The Extraterrestrial."

Yes. I'm sure that had something to do with it. I think it was just a colossal unfair blow to John Carpenter that ET was released at almost the exact same time, but that's the way it sometimes crumbles, cookie-wise. I mean you get these breaks, these terrible, terrible breaks and it's unfortunate. Eventually the film did sort of build up a cult following, and I was pleased to see that later on, he got the attention that he deserved because he put so much into it. He lost a great deal of opportunity by rolling the dice on that picture.

The Thing was odd for a blockbuster film in that there wasn't a female love interest?

That was a big thing. I remember that there was a lot of controversy over that. That there was no woman other than the rubber sex doll, and that's the way John wanted it. John wanted it to be a realistic work environment for these guys – he said "That's the way it is at these places. That's the way it's going to be. I don't want a female character in the story."

Which I think was the right choice, as it would've changed everything had there been a woman around, it would have added a love story element which wasn't necessary. Plus, I think it makes it far more terrifying when it's just a bunch of guys and dogs!

Some of the Scenes were filmed in Alaska – was it as cold as it looked?

It was filmed mostly in Los Angeles, on a sound stage. Then three weeks in a place called Hyder, Alaska. It's a pretty desolate place. Believe me. Freezing. I think it was 27 below one night when we filmed, and the hotel was a bus ride away.

They were tough conditions. The snow was over five feet high; the cold was intense. It was especially difficult for the crew. Actors get treated very differently than the crew. It was so cold - we'd film and then run to find the blankets that someone had brought along.

There was an unspoken rule in horror films to only show the monster fleetingly to keep the suspense up – but "The Thing" gets a lot of screen-time. And if anything, it was scarier for it. What are your thoughts?

Yes. I guess it was now that you mention it. John went for this, something that really penetrates your nightmares. And something with such a fantastic design – such a constantly changing design needed a lot of time on screen. Both John and Rob Bottin came up with this frightening monster that just… well if you weren't paranoid before you saw that movie, you were definitely paranoid after you saw it. I think in many ways the movie is about paranoia.

I think after that movie Rob left the business. I think that he only did that movie and he was really under the gun. Studios are big corporations and there's a lot of pressure from them. I've done a few big studio movies and they spend a lot of money and they don't let you off the hook. They keep the pressure on.

Creativity doesn't interest them - it's just, "Is the movie going to get done? Is it going to make money? Is it going to sell?" That's really what they care about.

I didn't really get to know Rob very well. He was around, he would be around the set, but it wasn't a very social event for him because of the pressure he was under.

Your own death scene was very violent!

They all were! I remember doing the stunt myself, being thrown around by a machine that we covered in rubber – I was the guy that froze when The Thing revealed itself, and instead of

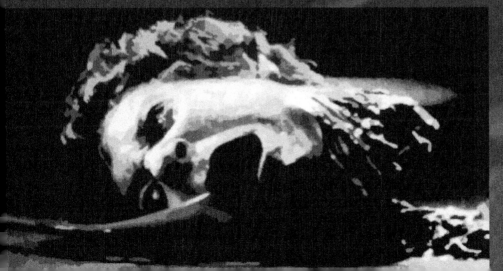

burning it with my flamethrower, I just stood there looking at it in amazement. I was picked up by my head and shaken, which wasn't the most comfortable experience I have ever had. But because I was in pretty good shape at the time, I could handle it. I got thrown around quite badly. But fortunately, only for a short time (on camera at least!), and I was thrown into a corner when The Thing gets distracted. The final version of my corpse was burnt before it could develop into another "Thing" properly so I was lucky – I didn't have to wear a lot of prosthetics, unlike one or two of the other actors – I just had to sit and twitch around in the corner for a while with something dumb stuck to my face.

You die a lot in films, don't you?

Yes. It seems so. TV shows too. I did an episode of Homeland last year and I get shot in the stomach, like five minutes into the story. In The Punisher on Netflix - oh my God, I die the most brutal death. They shove a broomstick down my throat. It's just horrifying.

I think I'm just the kind of guy that when you look at me, you instantly just want to kill me in really imaginative ways.

How do you think acting in plays differs to acting in movies?

I think acting in plays is far more difficult. There's no money, there's a lot of rehearsal, a lot of work.

Working in films, there's something magical because you know it's going to last forever. You know that they use that close-up, that particular moment when you were thinking about

your daughter, or your son, or whatever. That's an indelible print that you leave, for life. Unless the world ends, that print is going to be out there somewhere and somebody's going to see it and maybe they'll get what you were trying to convey.

I have my own acting studio. It came about way back in the '80s when I was doing American Buffalo with Al. An actor by the name of Vincent Pastore (who went on to become famous for playing Pussy in the Sopranos) was at that time a night club owner. He asked me to sign a poster after one of the shows. He said, "Tommy, I own a bar in Westchester, but my dream has always been to be an actor. How does somebody do that?" I said, "Well, you have to study. You have to train." He said, "Where do I go?" I said, "I don't know. There's a million schools around." He said, "Well, would you teach me?" I thought about it for a second. I didn't need the money at the time. I always knew I had a proclivity for teaching. So, I started my own acting classes, starting with Vinny. He was my

only student. Then three months later I had 35 or 40 students in the class. You have to try to never get caught acting. You have to make it sound like it's the first time it's ever been said. It's never been said by anyone else before and get to the point where you're not acting anymore. It's just your soul talking through a character. That can make you incredibly vital and interesting to watch.

Teaching has been good for me and I enjoy it so much. I'm not one of those embittered acting teachers that's never had any success. I'm still working as an actor. I'm still auditioning for roles. I'm still out there trying to get stuff done. Life goes on and you can only do the best that you can.

BIG
COUNTRY

Big Country made a huge impact upon my life. Great musicians, punchy rock music, but with a quiet and emotional side to them that appealed to myself as a teenager, and they also tapped into my vague folk leanings with their bagpipe sounding guitars. I still remember the excitement of hearing "Fields of Fire" and "In a Big Country" for the first time, and they have been on my "to play" list continually for the rest of my life.

Tragically Stuart Adamson committed suicide in 2000. The band limps on with various replacement lead singers but the magic has gone. But the music will always be with us.

Tony
Butler

Tony was the Bass Player and occasional song writer in the band, as well as playing with other great bands such as The Pretenders and various members of The Who as a session musician.

So how did the Tony Butler story begin?

I grew up in a little West London town called Shepherd's Bush and it was a typical multi-racial area back in those days. I started dabbling with musical instruments from the age of about, I should say, five, six – around the time when my Father died.

He'd bought me a piano and I plonked on that for about 10 minutes and decided I didn't like it - and I didn't really look at any other sort of instrument until I was about 10 when I suddenly got really into rock music, which was against the grain. Black kids back in those days were supposed to like reggae and such like! I started listening to Jimmy Hendrix. I'd pore over album sleeves and just dream that I would be in a band with him.

When I was in secondary school, I started learning how to play bass because of my music teacher, a guy called Ken Williams, who's a fantastic guy, a Welshman.

He asked us all in the class that if we were to play a musical instrument, what would we like to play? It just so happened, the previous night, I was watching Top of the Pops and there was Norman Greenbaum playing a song called, Spirit in the Sky. The camera did a close-up on a Fender Jazz Bass and I looked at it in wonderment and amazement, and I said, "I want one of those, I want to play one of those." So, my answer was "I would like to try the bass."

I was quite happy that I had something at my school that I could play.

I found that my musical taste was quite wide and varied, but It wasn't until I was a teenager that I actually ended up joining a band with my cousin who was in the army and was a bit of a singer. They had a soul band whilst they were in the Forces and he took me over to Germany where they were posted at the time, and I went over to do some gigs with them.

I stayed out there for three months just messing around on a bass guitar. It was soul music, and my real love was now rock, but he gave me a start.

My father had been a musician. He was originally a trumpet player on the island of Dominica where we originated from. He was regarded as a pop star, and my mum was a follower of his music… and they ended up marrying. They came over to England with my mum pregnant with me at the time.

You're first band was called On the Air, how did all that come about?

One of my school friends said that he had some friends who were looking to put a band together. I was about 13 years old at this time. I went around to a house in Ealing Common, West London, and I knocked on the door and this old, dishevelled lady answered the door, accused me of being a drug dealer, and told me to "fuck off!". I said, "No, I'm here to audition!" Then, she apologized and let me in.

The lady that had opened the door was Betty Townshend - Pete Townshend's mum. (Pete Townshend was in a band called The Who). Simon Townshend was Pete's younger brother and there was an older Townshend brother (who's about my age) called Paul. And these were the people that wanted to put a band together! We chose the name "Clear Blue Sky".

I began to hang around in that crowd and we started developing the band. The flavour of the day were bands like Genesis. We wanted to be like them because we wanted to play "intelligent" music.

We weren't into the three-minute ditties that constituted most of the chart music at the time. We were a five-piece and after about two years, we became a three-piece

and that's when we decided to make a clean break of it, and rename ourselves – and so the band "On the Air" was born.

The band, then, went on to become a sort of Simon Townshend vehicle. Simon Townshend himself started getting some interest from record companies (probably because of his name), and we went from being an autonomous group, to becoming Simon Townshend's backing band, which we didn't like very much because we didn't like the idea of trading on the name Townshend. To be fair, Simon himself didn't really want to do it but he had no option because that's the way that his parents and

Pete himself had promoted him. But Pete Townshend had our best interests at heart - Pete saw us as a new band struggling along and he gave us opportunities to develop. On one occasion, he invited us to his studio in Goring-on-Thames and he had just installed a quadraphonic system, and we were the first band to record using quadraphonic recording methods. That was a nice thing.

We started to Hang out at Pete's house too which was fantastic – as you would imagine, it's a shrine to The Who - gold, and platinum discs all over the walls. It was my idea of what the rock and roll lifestyle should be like, and I wanted to be part of that world.

We went from "On the Air", to "The Simon Townshend Band" but then, we went back to being "On the Air" again for some reason – and we finally got our own record deal with WA Records. We recorded a single with a producer called John Burns who was, at one time, the Genesis producer. He produced The Lamb Lies Down, I think. We thought that getting John was really, really

smart. We thought we were very cutting edge! A guy who was just a friend of ours became our manager and he managed to get us signed up for a tour with a Scottish band called, The Skids, which I hadn't really known much about. We weren't really part of the New Wave scene, as it was called, because we considered that that was a little bit beneath us.

Our introduction to The Skids was really important because we looked at ourselves differently to other emerging bands - and they themselves were something really different too. They were unaffected by anything in the music scene apart from what they themselves did.

I think that us being around them changed the way we thought about our music and our style, and rather than being a Genesis-influenced band, we slowly turned into a three-piece band with a more aggressive rock-pop attitude. And for this we needed a new drummer.

We held the auditions at the Shepperton Studios and we had about five or ten drummers turn up (we'd put an advert in Melody Maker). We were asking for a Phil Collins, Bill Bruford-type drummer despite the change in direction sound-wise.

Mark Brzezicki was one of the ones to audition, and he was brilliant. Such a clever drummer in more ways than one! Mark wangled himself to be the last one to be auditioned and what we didn't know at the time was, he was "earwigging" what the others were doing and the songs they were playing. By the time he came in, he was shit hot. It was as if he'd known the songs previously – he tricked us – but he was the best drummer too - we took him on from there. That's where my relationship with Mark started and we're still friends to this day.

You later joined Stuart Adamson in Big Country of course – what were your initial impressions?

I remember the first night of the tour with The Skids because it was just so awesome, for a few different reasons.

We turned up at the gig, it was at the Leicester Polytechnic called, the De Montfort Hall. I walked in and we were all really excited. There was a guy fiddling with bass guitars on the stage and I went up to him and said, "Hey, we're the support act. Where are we supposed to be?" This rather angry, Scottish person turned around and said, "Get out of my fucking way. "That person was actually, I found out subsequently, Russell Webb, The Skids bass player at the time.

I think we finally introduced ourselves. They let us have a sound check, which was nice of them, and we did our own gig very nervously. It was watching The Skids after our show that I really noticed Stuart. I thought he was an awesome guitarist, I thought he was incredibly unique in his guitar playing.

I loved the songs that I was hearing from The Skids. I didn't particularly like the vocalist though because I couldn't understand a word he was saying!

I didn't really take much note of the rest of the group because Stuart loomed so large in my head, he was just fantastic. As the tour went on, I made sure I got to know him a bit. He was a very quiet chap who, I learned, was very much into practical

jokes! We got on throughout the tour. He seemed to be the quiet, contemplative one, whereas, the others had a sort of New Wave aggression, particularly Jobson, the vocalist.

Russell Webb, I got to know because he was their bass player and I was our bass player. We spent about two or three weeks touring around Britain and it was a great, great atmosphere.

When the tour finished, I remember talking to Stuart and saying "Look, if you ever need a rhythm section, myself and Mark would probably be available." We had realised that Simon Townshend was being set up again to be a solo artist and I thought that the band was coming to an end, so I might as well start looking around for something else.

Then, low and behold, 18 months later, Stuart had left The Skids to create Big Country. Stuart had obviously remembered our chat because we got a call from Ian Grant (Big Country's Manager), who said "We'd like you to come down to Phonogram Studios and do some stuff."

I cheekily said, "Yes, how much are we getting paid?" - he told me to fuck off. Mark and I duly turned up at Phonogram Studios in London and it was just awesome. We set up our equipment and we listened to the songs that we were going to be playing, and it all sounded very different to what we were expecting.

The big shock was meeting Bruce Watson for the first time (because I just could not understand a single word he was saying!) His Scottish accent was so strong. Stuart obviously had a Scottish accent too which I'd now gotten

used to but Bruce was a different entity. I didn't talk to Bruce much because I didn't understand him!

When we finished recording the demo, I was trembling. Everything sounded so great – we'd played this song called, Heartless Soul and the bass line was absolutely fantastic, even if I do say so myself. At the end of the session, this guy from the record company had a listen to what we had just produced. He was just sitting there and he had a huge smile on his face.

I asked Stuart who he was and he said, "His name's Chris Briggs and he's the A&R man for Phonogram!" and by the end of the session, we had a record deal. Brilliant.

And when I say "we" it is because Big Country also signed me to the band and made an offer to Mark as well. (And we still haven't been paid for that session by the way…) Driving home from the session, I was saying to Mark, "I think we're onto something here," but Mark was very apprehensive…Mark is a drummer, he's married to his drums - drums mean everything to him. He loves playing with whoever wants him and felt a bit restricted to just play with the one band. I had to coerce him over the following period, to get him to agree to sign the contract.

And that was it - we were on our way as Big Country. But I had a previous commitment I had to uphold before we could get started. Before we got together to start rehearsing - I had to go and do a session that was previously booked, with The Pretenders. We recorded Back on the Chain Gang. Afterwards, I was asked if I wanted to join the band, but I had to turn it down because of my commitments to Big Country.

Big Country seemed to have instant success - was it really like that, though?

It was. It was exactly like that. The guys in the band came down from Scotland and lived at my house in West Ealing. We were writing songs, we were trying out ideas there, and then we went to rehearsals. It seemed like the very next minute, we were playing on bloody Top of the Pops!

It was all within six to 10 months, it was just extraordinary. It just took off and we were all quite bewildered. I think Stuart was a bit phased too, because although he'd known some success with The Skids, I don't think that he really understood how it happened so quickly with Big Country, or at least to the extent that it did.

What was the music writing like inside the band? Did you all have input?

I think the first song that we started looking at as a unit, rather than just learning stuff that Bruce and Stuart had done, was the track, The Crossing, eventually from the album of the same name. Because of myself and Mark's background, The Crossing was the nearest thing to what we had known as musicians previously, because of the elongated nature of the song - a song that had different parts, and was polyrhythmic. That's the place where Mark and I had come from, musically.

That really got us involved in the creation of the new music. We hadn't started writing songs at that time with the band, so this was the moment when we started to think that we could have a lot more input song writing-wise, although obviously Stuart and Bruce were still the main songwriters at that point. By the time we got to The Seer album, all of us were trotting out ideas for songs to work on. Stuart was really good - he'd listen to other ideas.

The album, Steeltown, had a much different atmosphere to The Crossing. you trying to get away from the rockier sound of before?

I don't know. I think consciously, we knew we wanted to write an album that was The Crossing - part two, but I think it was the world politically then was quite bleak, and everything seemed quite glum. Also, after two years of bashing out The Crossing, and touring around the world, we were all fucked, completely. We were tired. Stuart especially was, just wasted, empty. Going back into the studio to start writing, and rehearsing new stuff, I think, was a bit too soon for us.

THEN we had to go and start working on the new album. That was a real chore, I think, for all of us and I think that's why the album took on that grey complexion.

You had some hits in America but why do you think you as a band, Big Country never really took off there?

It didn't take off purely and simply because Stuart was very difficult to deal with, at that time. We knew that we had an opportunity to go and break America. Obviously, U2 had just done that, and it had opened the door to other rock bands from the UK, but I think that Stuart's problems were really starting to manifest around then. He would go missing, couldn't be contacted. Anything that the management were trying to organize, ended up being thwarted.

The Crossing stayed in the charts for a long time in the USA, but the Americans didn't really take to Steeltown. I felt that the success was still there for us to take, but we had to make a big effort. And it just didn't happen - it's a regret that Stuart didn't rise to the opportunity to really hammer home what we, as a band, had done already there.

What do you think contributed to Stuart's problems? Was it just the pressure, do you think?

Yes, the pressure, alcohol. Although he was the lead in the front line, he didn't enjoy it, he didn't relish being in that position. He just wanted to be a writer and a singer, and play his guitar. He loved being on stage, he loved playing, but of all the rest of the stuff, he didn't like the fame and dealing with the day to day problems…

His personal problems, alcohol problems, they all started to really develop between the end of The Crossing and I think, up to The Seer. By the time we had completed The Seer, he was a bit more with it and we were writing really good stuff again. We then started having record company problems by that time. Again, another aggravating pressure.

It was to do with the A&R (Artists and Repertoire Manager). It was Chris Briggs, who was the original A&R. Of course, he was very supportive. He supported us through the whole Polar Studios, Sweden recordings of Steeltown, but he then subsequently left. We were taken over by Dave Bates, who made his name as an A&R man bringing Tears for Fears to the world. He thought he was the bee's knees and we hated him. We had nothing in common with him and our relationship didn't just break down. It completely cracked up.

The Seer, was being produced by Robin Miller - he brought a poppy element to our sound, which we loved, and we got on really well with him. We felt he was right for us. We'd finished recording it, we were back on the road touring. Then we were told, literally, while we were on the bus that he had been sacked and they'd drafted in some guy that we didn't know to mix the album. This guy was called, Walter Talbott... Then, we started hearing all these horror stories that he was replacing our guitars, getting other people to do guitar overdubs and stuff.

There was a lot of fear and frustration for us because we were on the road and couldn't step in to fix the situation. Relations were strained between ourselves and our management, as well. It was just horrible.

Big Country have been accused of musically not evolving – and "all Big Country records sound the same" – Do you think that you can't really win? If you did sound different you were criticised and if you didn't you were also criticised.

I agree with that completely because you strive to be creative. You strive to move yourself forward as an individual, as a writer, in life, in general, and you try to do what you do best. I think that we fell into the trap of having such a defined sound. If we did the same thing all the time, you get ripped for that and if you try something different and you didn't sound like what you originally sounded like, you're not part of the game anymore.

That was a struggle but at the end of the day, we were happier trying to be creative. In fact, it was the way we were individually evolving as musicians that was starting to cause us problems.

We were sort of drifting apart musically by then. We mainly saw ourselves collectively as a loud guitar rock band, which suited myself and Bruce. But individually, Stuart's affinity deep down was to Country and Western. And Mark just wanted to be both Phil Collins and Bill Bruford as a drummer. I won't say we started drifting apart at that exact point but all of the pressures surrounding it began to encroach - particularly, the alcohol. That was the biggest problem.

Actually, I think it was just before we started recording The Seer, both Stuart and Bruce declared that they were alcoholics and they were attending AA. We wanted to support them as much as we could because we were also friends at this time. We need to support people.

It certainly had a bearing on how we were going to be as humans and how we were going to be as a band, which is why that whole period became really quite difficult. After The Seer had finished, after we'd worked it out, and published it, it didn't feel complete. I felt we had done less work on the album. I felt that some of the enthusiasm had gone from the band.

What happened to trigger the eventual end of the band?

It was when we were recording, Driving to Damascus. Stuart seemed to be in good shape. We were all into the songs that we'd put together for that and we were all enjoying recording. Then, when we got to the mixing stage, Stuart felt that it was a job done. He'd done his part, and it was now up to the producers and whoever else was interested to complete the album and to get it into the shops. At this point in time, he'd moved home to Nashville. So, he went back there after the recording sessions were completed, but we stayed and carried on mixing.

Once Stuart had left, we were informed by one of the studio cleaners that Stuart's room had been "a shrine to alcohol". We didn't even think he was drinking but the room was full of bottles, beer cans, all sorts of things. We realized then that he was actually in really bad shape, and had been hiding it from us. Sometime later, we were contacted by somebody who had seen Stuart in a bar

- he'd passed out on a table covered in empty bottles. I was more intent that he just went and got himself fixed and sorted out. By then the band was secondary. He needed help. But the final crack that eventually destroyed the band came externally - it was when we released a new single, Fragile Thing.

We were all really excited about it as a single because, to me, it was Radio Two fodder and we needed that exposure on a major radio station to climb back to where we had been before and to recover all the ground we'd lost over the intervening years.

We had Eddi Reader (vocalist in the band "Fairground Attraction") doing some guest vocals on it. And it sold really well! Our record company informed us were heading to the charts once again! Everyone was really happy and optimistic. It was a great moment. I felt that things were going great again, and we were back to being the old Big Country once more.

Then a few days later, we had a catastrophe! We were informed by the chart organization (the people that put the record charts together), that they had stopped registering one of the fancier formats of the CDs that we were using from the sales total, and would be striking off those figures. This format was an open jewel case that had a booklet inside it, and had the bulk of our sales. I supposed they felt it was cheating in a way.

It was obviously devastating news for us. It went from being a Top 40 single to barely reaching number 70 overnight. It had a really bad effect on everybody, because we went from knowing we had another hit in the charts again, to such low depths. This

particularly must have affected Stuart because he disappeared again, and I knew that the end was on the cards, then.

We continued to tour to promote the new material though, we were contractually obliged, and I had a bit of a summit meeting with Stuart who had resurfaced by this time. I think we were in Germany. I went to his room in the hotel and I had a heart-to-heart with him. I said, "You need to go and get yourself sorted out. Even if it means me leaving to break up the band, to force you to stop - that's what I'm willing to do, because you're not in a good place."

And that's what happened. Basically, after that tour, to all intents and purposes, I'd left the band. It wasn't something that I was going to publicize or make an announcement about though, and I never saw Stuart again until months later.

We were invited to play at a concert in Malaysia. I was tempted back into playing with the band again because this was quite a good money-maker for us all, and to be honest, individually, we were all getting a bit skint by then. We thought "It's just a money gig. But let's do this and then see where we go as a band."

But when we all arrived in Kuala Lumpur, we'd discovered that Stuart wasn't there. We feared the worse. What had happened was, he was drunk, and he had left his flight early and ended up getting off in Japan rather than Kuala Lumpur. We still had time to get him to the gig though, and we put the wheels in motion to get him onto another flight. By the time we got him to Kuala Lumpur, he'd continued to drink en route, and he was in a mess. The subsequent gig, went ahead though, and, for me, was a complete and utter embarrassment. He didn't know where he was, he didn't know what he was doing. He was completely screwed.

And then after the gig, we assumed that was that. I was never to see Stuart again. Then of course, he disappeared for the final time, we asked fans to contact us if they knew where he was — we were worried about him - and then we later discovered that he had committed suicide in a hotel room in Hawaii.

Since Big Country you've worked on a few solo albums — do you feel you've gone back to your roots with a much rockier sound?

The band continues to this day but to me, the dream was gone when Stuart died. I got pulled back into the band on a couple of occasions but that was just to help out my colleagues, the manager, and stuff.

By the time I actually left them for good, which was in 2012, I decided that the band was completely finished and it was my time to write something to show the world what I can do, this is my time, in terms of where I am in my own life.

I started my own record company in Cornwall to help young bands. I released a couple of albums on my label. My latest album My Time. is the first album that I want to stand up and be counted by. I put a lot of effort into it, I play everything on it, apart from drums, and to me, it's my best as a songwriter. But I always wanted to help the new generations of musicians coming through too.

Did your new career as a teacher stem from wanting to help young people with your studio?

Yes, it was, again, around the time when I knew the band was coming to an end and I needed to think about my future. I really enjoyed what I did throughout my career, but, even more, my record label was like a form of teaching. I wanted to do that in a more traditional sense. In 2002, I had qualified. I earned a degree and I ended up teaching in a college in Barnstaple.

To me, that was the best place for me to be in my time and experience, and I loved it. I really got off on being able to show people the way because I'd done it.

I thought it was a very unselfish gesture but it was also a job. I wanted to leave the music industry and all the hassles that go with it. I didn't want to join up with other musicians my age and be part of any super group, I didn't want to tour anymore, I didn't want do anything like that because my time doing that was with Big Country and those days were over.

Things evolve in life, and not just the music, and sometimes it's just time to do something new.

131

Stewart Lee and Richard Herring came together at University in the 1980s as a comedy duo, moved to London and began to write for lots of humour filled radio shows, which eventually led to "Fist of Fun" that first aired in 1992 – It qualifies as a 1980s entry in the book, as I first discovered the partnership on radio in the 1980s, although I know it is cheating a little…

Fist of Fun was the first TV show since The Young Ones (shown ten years earlier), that really made me laugh – the alternative comedy scene was getting dull and jaded, and way too political, and it was nice to get a more traditional comedy team on the screen again. Don't get me wrong – they were original enough with their writing and delivery to still thumb their noses at mainstream comedy, whilst still embracing it or creating ironic takes on it. It was truly marvellous

Richard Herring

Richard played the cheeky, puerile one in the partnership, and was great comic relief to the more cynical and often cruel persona of Stewart Lee. Often faux naïve, or incredulous to the given situation, it was a delightful performance, that you couldn't help but laugh at.

What sort of humour / TV shows / Comedians did you like when you were younger? Was there a certain type of comedy that you gravitated towards?

I was obsessed with funny people from a young age. My grandad made me laugh and I loved anyone who had that magical power. On TV I liked the anarchy of programmes like the Banana Splits and The Goodies and especially Tiswas. I cried when we moved to Somerset and discovered Tiswas wasn't shown in the region. Then as I got older, I got into Monty Python and Derek and Clive via the LPs and then The Young Ones was a huge influence on me. So, anarchy and smartass stuff were my preference, though I ate up all Light Entertainment and remember laughing till it hurt at Cannon and Ball, for example.

When did you first start to harbour dark thoughts about becoming involved in comedy yourself? Were you the class joker, or did it all happen later on?

I was always interested in trying to make people laugh and messed around in class (whilst finding the work pretty easy and also being academic, making me doubly annoying). It didn't seem possible to go into comedy as a job in 1980s Somerset (my careers advisor scoffed at the idea of me working as a writer or performer), but we did sketch shows at school and I wanted to go to Oxford so I could do comedy like the people I'd read about in shows such as Fringe and Monty Python's Flying Circus. Also, my brother's best friend from school, Bill Matthews had started working on the satirical radio show "Weekending", so I knew, despite what my career's advisor said, it was possible to escape Somerset, and go to London and do this as a job.

How did you meet Stewart Lee? And did you click immediately?

We sort of nearly met a few times in the first term at University, but passed in corridors or fast food shops lots of times. The weeks I appeared at the comedy club and tried out my first routines,

he didn't go, and then I had exams at the end of the first term so had to concentrate on those and hadn't really got involved in the club when he was on stage. But we'd heard about each other and liked the sound of what we'd both individually been doing and finally met at the Christmas party for the comedy club in a cricket pavilion. I was pogoing to the Sex Pistols which impressed him and then we made up stories about the ancient cricket teams in the photos on the walls. As everyone else was just doing very Pythonesque sketches, our stuff sounded a bit different (I had a sketch about having a singing penis and he did one about people holding fruit at a bus stop) we decided to collaborate.

We were always united by finding the same things funny and made a list of rules of stuff we wouldn't do – TV parodies, celebrity-based humour etc and so yes, I think we did click comedically immediately. It was a fun and productive time as we wrote ten minutes of new sketches every fortnight for the next two terms and then had a show to take to Edinburgh.

thought and realised that if a philosophy does not allow you to question it, then there is only one reason for that – it's shit! So, there was a bit of anarchy and rebellion and no doubt a little nod to Life of Brian in there too somewhere. Obviously, Stew took it one step further, with "Jerry Springer, The Opera" …

How did you meet Kevin Eldon, and how did he become part of the show?

He was on the stand-up circuit and pally with Stew especially. We both loved his act but he was treading water a bit and not using his talents to their full extent. Basically though, we were doing a radio show in Exeter and no one wanted to travel that far for bad money to do the sketches with us. He said, "I'll do it". He absolutely got what we were doing and was able to do our characters way better than we'd have been able to and especially understood the

After that, we came to London and did stand up separately, but worked together on scripted stuff on shows like "Weekending" and then "On The Hour", as well as other bits and pieces for TV/radio and things that never got made.

I first became aware of you when you started to appear on Fist of Fun, how did you get the breakthrough from stand-up to then go and do radio and then TV?

After the success of On the Hour and a bit of a struggle and our producer threatening to resign, we got our own radio show, "Lionel Nimrod's Inexplicable World". Some of these were then repeated on Radio 1 who wanted us to come up with shows for them. Fist of Fun came out of that.

Then of course it became very popular and we ended up having our own TV show – Fist of Fun once again. From there, we did "This Morning, with Richard not Judy". Both shows were on TV at odd times of the day, something we actually joked about on the show, but both had a decent enough following.

How did you go about writing sketches together? Was there a rough process to it all?

We were young and fizzing with ideas and didn't really have a defined process. Sometimes we wrote a sketch individually and then messed around with it together and sometimes we sat together and hammered it out (and spent hours arguing over a word sometimes). We spent a lot of time watching TV. "The Shrewsbury Pie Pie" was basically a piss take of a poor documentary that came on after Neighbours one day. Sometimes we took a subject and researched it a bit – which meant going to a library in those days. But we (especially me) worked very hard and comedy was our (especially my) main focus.

Religion, and all of its many inconsistencies was the focal point to a lot of your humour – was this simply because there is a lot to laugh about? Did you ever feel a bit guilty about it?

I'd been brought up in a mildly religious house and was religious as a kid and occasionally worried we might be smited or smote by God. But both myself and Stew had rebelled against any doctrinal comedy of obsession (hence the sketches with the "Simon Quinlank – King of Hobbies") and so on, which we were ironically obsessed with. So, it was an obvious fit.

You've written for lots of TV shows and plays – do you find you like writing for yourself more than for others? Can writing for others have its frustrations?

Yes of course – I've written for several radio shows, and also worked with Al Murray on "Time Gentlemen Please". Like any job it has its ups and downs. See my blog from 12th Feb to see how frustrating writing can be. I like writing, but am at my best when in control of a project, so stand-up or a sitcom that is my baby where I am happiest (though all writing makes me quite unhappy until it is over). I'd rather do my own thing, I think. My recent experiences have cemented that resolve. I continue to tour and I have a successful podcast series too.

What did your family think of you having a career in comedy?

They've been very supportive – I think partly because they were less supportive of my older siblings' dreams and realised it was better to actually let your kids try and fail than to stop them trying. So, they like it. But my dad thinks I should pay him for all the stuff of his that I just repeated verbatim.

You're still performing and still as popular as ever – do you think you'll ever retire?

No, I think I will die in the saddle. Illness aside there's no need to retire from this job, but I have been making an effort (not entirely successfully) to slow down a bit and spend more time with my family.

Printed in Great Britain
by Amazon